Making Vintage

1930s

CLOTHES FOR WOMEN

Ciara Phipps and Claire Reed

THE CROWOOD PRESS

First published in 2018 by
The Crowood Press Ltd
Ramsbury, Marlborough
Wiltshire SN8 2HR

www.crowood.com

British Library Cataloguing-in-Publication Data
A catalogue record for this book is available from the British Library.

ISBN 978 1 78500 501 5

All photographs © Tessa Hallmann Photography

Dedications
Ciara: For Oran, Mum and Agnes.
Claire: This book is dedicated to the memory of my grandmothers, Daisy and Nora; also to Mum, my one-woman PR machine, and to my husband Clive, who always tells me how proud he is of me.

Typeset by Sharon Dainton Design
Printed and bound in India by Parksons Graphics

Contents

Introduction

Wearing vintage clothing is often an alluring and enticing prospect, given the variety of exciting styles, shapes and fabrics available to recreate historic looks. Making vintage-inspired clothing allows the maker to engage with the different construction techniques that were used historically, the variety of dynamic patterns and shapes that were worn, and the magic associated with fashion from previous decades. Whether you are making garments for yourself or as a commission for someone else, the opportunity to embrace the elegance and sensual nature of clothing from the 1930s will encourage you to view clothing with a greater appreciation for its construction.

Embed elegance into your personal style by taking inspiration from the 1930s.

The wearable nature of fashion from the 1930s will allow you to create your own individual and unique look, one that accentuates and celebrates the shape of the female body. Both elegant and functional, thirties style is timeless and very translatable to the contemporary wearer. By incorporating garments inspired by or based on original thirties clothing into your own look, you can capture the 'chicness' inherent in fashion from this fascinating era. The lasting appetite for both wearing and making vintage clothing comes partly from the unrivalled quality of early to mid-twentieth-century clothing. Whether ready-to-wear or couture, clothing made during the 1930s was of extremely high quality in its construction and finishing. This element of quality assurance gives the contemporary wearer and maker an understanding and appreciation for the importance of this quality when creating a timeless garment made to stand the test of time.

This book explores the history of 1930s clothing by unpicking the styles, designers and context of the era, providing a platform for you to understand how fashion from this decade developed, before moving on to learn how to reproduce your very own thirties-inspired garments. With instructions, patterns and photos, it looks at and celebrates the elegant fluidity of thirties fashion and the classic nature of the garments selected for re-creation in this book.

The 1930s was a time of crisis, conflict and upheaval; however, fashion, art and design flourished, providing a foundation on which designers could expand and develop after the end of World War II. The figure-hugging nature of clothing from the thirties and the development of activewear both demonstrate the change in body image and issues of social morality. A decade of liberation for women, the thirties is often called upon as inspiration for many contemporary designers. The bias cut will forever be a timeless feature of fabric manipulation and draping, something many designers and makers utilize today in order to achieve fluidity, sensuality and movement in the garments they are creating.

The beauty of vintage clothing is in its uniqueness.

Although hugely adaptable and wearable for the contemporary reader or maker, the interest and continuing

A woman with cropped shingled hair wearing a luxurious coat with fur-edged lapels and cuffs, riding a horse with a sophisticatedly dressed man in a trench coat and matching hat. Gap of Dunloe Killarney, 1930. (Ciara Phipps' family photo)

Left: Summer day dress.

Three young women wearing mid-calf length woollen skirts with cropped blazers and short bobbed hair. The central woman wears a double-breasted cropped jacket, while the woman on the left of the photo has low slung buttons with wide decorative button holes, 1935. (Ciara Phipps' family photo)

designs to choose from, whilst also focusing on garments that can be translated to contemporary tastes and figures.

The patterns are taken from original 1930s garments and have been carefully measured and are accurate to within approximately 1.2cm (½in). The measurements are non-standard, as each garment was bespoke-made for the individual wearer, and are for guidance only; however, they have been compared to current sizing standards as much as possible. It is always good practice to take accurate measurements of the individual for whom the garment is being made and the historical silhouettes portrayed in the patterns may require adapting for the modern body shape.

All the patterns are fully annotated with a scale clearly visible on each. Some patterns will have two differing scales from which to work: the garments chosen for the book vary greatly in type, style and cut, so it was necessary to scale in this manner to fit the book. It will be clear which patterns this applies to.

Measurements are given in both metric and imperial sizes to suit individual preference. The patterns that consist of more than one sheet are clearly identified at the top of each pattern page. The patterns are for guidance and will require re-sizing to individual measurements.

Unless otherwise stated, seam allowances have not been included, so this must be considered when laying out and cutting the pattern pieces. A recommended allowance is 1.2 cm (½in).

The step-by-step instructions which accompany each individual pattern are accompanied by images of the original garments which show their construction in more detail. It is worth taking the time to study the pattern and instructions before beginning your sewing project and it may, in some cases, be beneficial to create a toile before the actual garment is cut, to allow for adaptations and adjustments to be carried out.

When calculating the fabric

love of thirties clothing is in its uniqueness. Whether you are looking to simply enhance your capsule wardrobe with some unique one-of-a-kind thirties garments to pair with contemporary clothing and accessories, or whether you are keen to embrace and redefine your look with a thirties twist, there are plenty of beautiful examples within this book to recreate and reinterpret.

The garments included in this book are from the dress and textiles collection held at Southend Museums Service. This collection is vast and varied and includes examples of costume and accessories dating from the seventeenth century onwards. This collection also contains the largest and most comprehensive collection of swimwear in the country, which was a wonderful resource when researching

the development of activewear and resort wear in the thirties. The collection of 1930s clothing within the collection is both diverse and dynamic, ensuring that a varied selection has been included here, allowing the reader to create a complete thirties-inspired capsule wardrobe. Given their unlimited access, the authors have been able to get up close and personal with each garment explored in this book.

The book begins with a lingerie set and moves through to a coat, and includes all the garments in between that would make up a classic 1930s wardrobe. With twelve extensive patterns, each chapter contains a garment or set of garments to make one outfit that can be reproduced or reinterpreted. This provides a good variety of thirties shapes, styles and

Four fashionable women on the beach, wearing examples of summer resort wear. The structured shoulders suggest these garments are from the late 1930s. The woman on the far left of the image is wearing high waist shorts, possibly even a small playsuit with a cinched in waist. Lillian Greaney and family at the beach, late 1930s. (Ciara Phipps' family photo)

quantities for the garments described in this book, it is always prudent to err on the generous side with fabric quantities, especially those cut on the bias grain and those patterns using facings, bindings and decorative elements cut from the garment fabric.

The patterns in this book have been aimed at the experienced seamstress, but the step-by-step instructions that accompany them have been written in as clear and concise a manner as possible, in order to encourage the home dressmaker with a good general knowledge of sewing techniques. Some of the patterns may appear to be more complicated than they actually are, but by meticulously ordering the pattern pieces and carefully following the step-by-step instructions, hints and tips, creating your own 1930s garment is definitely achievable. There will also be some inspirational suggestions on how to update each vintage garment for the contemporary wearer, with some contemporary accessories or details you might want to consider when creating your own 1930s-inspired wardrobe.

Daisy Thompson in the garden of her family home in Poplar, East London c.1935. Daisy's brothers and father are dressed in typical working class wear. Daisy wears a polka dot patterned dress with fancy ruched collar. Her sister is in a lightweight summer dress and their mother wears a wrap-over style dress with embellished fold down collar. (Claire Reed's family photo)

Creating Your 1930s Garment

Making your own clothing is a very satisfying experience and one which allows the seamstress to let her imagination run free with the endless choice of fabric types and dazzling array of fabric colours, patterns and embellishments with which to create a truly unique and personal piece.

The 1930s is synonymous with sophistication and glamour, with its stylish and flattering cuts and opulent fabrics. The patterns in this book cover the classic staples of the 1930s wardrobe; from silky, figure-hugging evening dresses to smart, tailored daywear, they are projects aimed to inspire and encourage creativity.

Typically with this era of decadence and glamour, the fabrics used in the garments of the time reflect this, but can prove challenging to cut and stitch; however, with care and patience there is no reason why your project should not be successful and you will impress with your stylish attire. Imagine the feeling you'd have arriving at a special occasion enrobed in the soft, sensual blue velvet evening dress, or attending an interview clad head to toe in tailored crêpe de chine with sassy matching cape. The clothing we choose to wear can give us confidence when we feel we need it, express our individuality in a world of conformity or can simply be 'just because …'.

The best advice would be to make your first vintage sewing project the one where you feel most confident in your abilities to handle the fabric and cut of the piece. Certain fabrics are more forgiving than others and some of the patterns, such as the kimono robe, are simpler in cut and design and so will be straightforward to make. The garments described in the book are a combination of professional and home-made and have imperfections and unique methods of cut and stitching; basically they reflect the individuals who created them.

Below are hints and tips on the main fabric types and cuts used in the original garments: these may help when choosing your sewing project.

Working with Velvet

Velvet is a beautiful and luxurious fabric, but one which perennially fills the dressmaker, however experienced, with dread. This is down to the fact that it often proves tricky to work with due to its smooth, silky pile (nap) which can make it slide when stitching sections together. It also has a tendency to mark easily. Combined with the fact that it is virtually impossible to press with an iron, these attributes make it understandably off-putting to use. However, velvet has a luminosity that enhances even the simplest of styles, and the variety of velvet types available, from the smooth and lustrous silk velvets to the bold and tactile crushed velvets, are enough to encourage the dressmaker to give them a try.

With any dressmaking project, preparation is the key and this is particularly important when working with velvet fabrics. Take your time, ask or seek advice and the old adage of 'measure twice, cut once' is never as appropriate as with this fabric. When preparing to cut out the pattern pieces using a velvet fabric, the main thing to remember is that it has a defined direction of pile and care must be taken to place all the pattern pieces with the pile running in the same direction on each. Cutting sections of your garment with the pile running in different directions will result in shading, where the pieces almost appear to be of different hues.

To test the direction of the pile, run your hand up and down over the surface of the fabric; it will feel smooth as you push the fibres in one direction and coarse as you push them in the other. There are no hard and fast rules as to which direction the pile should run on the garment, but generally garments are made with the pile running down. Some dressmakers prefer to use the upward pile, as it provides a richer tone to the finished garment.

Avoid pinning velvet where possible and use fabric weights to hold the pattern pieces in place for cutting. Work on the reverse (wrong) side as much as possible and transfer the lines of the pattern using tailor's chalk or similar marker. If tacking, make sure the stitches are not pulled up too tightly as the fabric will mark.

When it comes to stitching using the sewing machine, there are some helpful tips to make this a little easier. Using a walking foot or reducing the force of the standard pressure foot will help ease guiding the fabric layers through the machine. A universal (sharp) machine needle of 70/10H or 80/12H will work best with this fabric and using a silk or cotton thread with a looser tension will benefit when sewing.

Velvet fabrics cannot be pressed in the conventional manner and so follow the guidelines in the book on pressing velvet fabrics, which are with the instructions for the velvet evening dress and the velvet evening jacket.

Left: Velvet evening dress.

Daisy Thompson on a seaside holiday c.1937. Daisy wears a short-sleeved floral summer dress with contrasting white belt. Worn with sandals and ankle socks and accessorized with a clutch bag and small hat, the outfit exudes a relaxed and youthful appearance. (Claire Reed's family photo)

folded double.

Only use fine, sharp pins and slide them carefully into the fabric weave and through the layers. Placing tissue paper between the fabric layers can help. When stitching using the sewing machine, always use a brand new, sharp needle of fine gauge, such as 60/8 or 70/10, depending on the fabric type. To help guide the fabric through the machine and avoid it being pulled into the foot plate, it is advisable to increase the force of the pressure foot and hold the fabric taut when guiding it along.

The general rule of thumb is to use a looser tension with a short stitch. Also, try to avoid back-stitching at the end of a run or seam, as this can cause the fabric to pull and pucker; simply tie off the threads to secure the end of the row of stitching. Use a sewing thread that is not too strong for the fabric and although a polyester thread is usually fine to use, a cotton thread is the ideal choice for fine fabrics.

A French seam is often the preferred choice in garments made from fabrics of this nature, due to the fact that, as it encloses the raw edges, the seam is neat and strong.

When pressing a fine fabric, take care to set the heat of the iron to suit the fabric type; in general terms, natural fibres such as silks can take a hotter iron setting than a synthetic fibre. It is always beneficial to use a clean pressing cloth and it is also worth testing a scrap of the chosen fabric as, with certain types, the heat can create unwanted surface shine. It is best to press fine fabrics on the reverse (wrong) side and avoid, where possible, pressing the right side.

Working with the Bias Grain

The bias grain runs at a 45-degree angle to the straight grain (warp and weft threads of the weave) and is often referred to as the 'cross' grain due to the fact that it runs diagonally across the straight grain of the fabric. Bias-cut garments offer excellent stretch and movement, creating a smooth and flattering silhouette and a close fit to

Working with Fine Fabric

The ethereal qualities of fine fabrics, such as silks, chiffon and other sheers, give a soft and romantic feel to a garment; they are light and comfortable to wear but not so easy to sew. Common problems encountered when working with these types of fabrics are fraying, puckering and pulling of the fibres; also they can be difficult to lay out when preparing for cutting.

Luxury fabrics come with a price tag to match and this can add to the anxiety and reluctance to use them. Fraying is an issue and some fabrics of this type have a tendency to fray more than others; as it is impossible to avoid handling when cutting, preparing and making up the garment there can be substantial loss to seam allowances if not done with great care. A useful tip is to ensure that scissors are sharp and free of nicks to the blades, which could snag the fabric fibres when cutting out the pattern pieces.

Take time when laying out fine fabrics and positioning the pattern pieces on them. As they have a tendency to move and distort during handling, be as gentle as possible. Ensure your hands are clean, and remove any chunky jewellery that may rub against the fabric and snag it. Rather than pulling at the fabric to manipulate it, try to lift, smooth and pat the surface to help it lie flat and even, especially when the fabric is the body. This method of cutting worked perfectly for the fluid and figure-hugging styles of 1930s garments; the stretch qualities meant that potentially bulky plackets and fastenings were not required as the garment could be slipped on over the head.

If you are inexperienced with this method of constructing garments, it is advisable to start off with a simple pattern and a fabric that has good weight and draping qualities. Avoid choosing a pattern that requires accurate matching at the seams or distinct patterns within the fabric design; the satin evening dress and cape, for example, requires several panels to be matched perfectly to achieve the crisp, geometric look of the piece and also uses a decorative finish on the hem that needs a skilled hand to produce.

The lingerie set might be a good starting point, as the pattern pieces are smaller and therefore easy to manipulate, plus the well-placed lace elements on the garments will distract from any mistakes, which dressmakers of any experience will tell you can easily happen.

The essential point to remember is to take care when laying out the pattern at the start of your project, as it is important to ensure that the direction of the grain lines on the pattern pieces are true. Cutting slightly off the bias grain will cause the pattern pieces to twist and make accurate stitching of the seams more difficult to achieve. Taking time at this stage will pay dividends when it comes to stitching the pattern pieces. Depending on the fabric type, it can be useful to use the single-layer method of laying out the pattern, especially where a silky fabric, such as a satin, is being used.

When cutting out the pattern pieces, a rotary tool works well and can make this process easier. If using scissors, ensure they are sharp; with particularly slippery fabrics, it is worth considering using scissors with serrated blades, as these give greater contact with the fabric.

Once the pattern pieces are cut, try not to over-handle them as they will stretch and distort. Use a light touch and lift the individual pieces gently, working on a flat surface where the fabric will be supported as it is being manipulated. It is advisable, where possible, to tack the garment seams before stitching as this will give the garment stability when it is guided through the sewing machine.

Use a machine needle recommended for fine fabrics as described in the previous section, and pull the fabric gently as it is guided under the pressure foot. For curved areas, such as a neckline, or if the fabric is particularly stretchy, running a row of stay-stitches can help to hold the shape and prevent distortion.

When it comes to creating the hem on the garment, it is worth leaving the garment to hang overnight, as gravity will pull the fibres downwards and it is best to let that happen before the garment is finished, in order to avoid an uneven hem. When pressing the finished garment, use the heat setting appropriate to the fabric type and make sure the garment does not hang and therefore pull at the seams. Lift and support the fabric when pressing.

There is much literature and online tutorial advice available in the world of sewing and crafting which are worth investigating and with the hints and tips offered in this book, we hope you will be inspired to create your own masterpiece. It is always a good idea to test out a fabric for its cutting and stitching qualities before embarking on your chosen sewing project and many fabric shops sell in small quantities, so it is worth investing in a couple of twenty-centimetre pieces to practise on and see what might suit your project.

Above all, enjoy making whatever it is that enthuses you; in whichever fabric, colour or pattern ignites your imagination!

Fashion History and Context

3

Socio-politically speaking, the 1930s can be framed by two major world events. The Wall Street Crash of 1929, followed by the outbreak of WWII just ten years later, led to the 1930s being overlooked in some areas of art, design and fashion study.

As one might imagine, such major events created a period of crisis for those living through the decade; however, the output of fashion designers, artists and architects would suggest the period was in fact a fruitful decade of flourishing creativity and innovation. According to some commentators on the period, the horrors of the war played a very big role in overshadowing the developments and changes in 1930s design and style. For many the period is defined by these major world events; however, the developments within the fashion and art world should not be underestimated. In a decade that followed on from the excesses of the Jazz Age, and preceded the era of austerity experienced in the utilitarian forties, the 1930s has, at times, been considered merely a transitional decade bridging the gap from one era of extremes to another. In fact, the 1930s witnessed some of the most interesting and innovative changes that still influence contemporary design and fashion today, something that more fashion historians, designers and authors are acknowledging.

The decade began with the 1929 Wall Street Crash, something that in many ways characterized the 1930s. This financial event was the largest collapse of the stock market in American and global history. The crash plunged the USA into the 'Great Depression' and left the world reeling from the ramifications of 'Black Tuesday', 29 October 1929. As the new decade began, everyone was swiftly becoming aware, often painfully, about the extent of this financial disaster in both America and Europe, in which 'Thrift is the spirit of the day. Reckless spending is a thing of the past' (as noted by the Sears catalogue for 1930). Levels of unemployment soared, and hardship and poverty proliferated. This depression and the severely high levels of unemployment persisted throughout the whole decade, regardless of the efforts nations made to curb the severity of the economic downturn. This festering financial disaster created the perfect breeding ground for new powers to take hold and sell a new way of life to those disheartened by the effects of the Great Depression. The rise of European authoritarian regimes was the result of this economic downturn experienced around the world. Before the end of the decade, Europe found itself embroiled in a horrifying conflict once again, one that would be remembered as the most shocking obliteration of life that Western history would experience. The foundation for WWII was laid in the 1930s, which perhaps led to the decade being viewed through a lens of negativity.

The preceding decade was considerably more fruitful in its excess of luxury and glamour, among many other things. The liberation and freedoms of women were a major item on the agenda, and the clothing of the time reflected this. The glitzy evening dresses of the 1920s were designed for the hedonistic lifestyles of a generation who grew up during the gloomy and oppressive years of WWI. These heavy years had restricted their fun and freedom and many in the middle and upper classes sought relief from the horrifying destruction and loss of life in nightclubs, impromptu parties and casual and frenzied socializing. There was a desire to reject the traditional ideals of the previous generations, thus there was a loosening of morals and clothing. Women had gained more economic social and political freedom which was reflected in a less fussy and restrictive modern wardrobe. The fashion of the twenties was comfortable, simplified and young-looking, with curves being outlawed and the tubular dress being worn with a dropped waist, a flattened bust and a straight silhouette.

Towards the end of the 1920s the waistline started to move back to its natural position, and the look of evening wear was considerably more elegant and mature with a traditionally 'feminine' silhouette beginning to appear. This clear refinement of clothing is considered a response to the Great Depression; however, the changes in fashion at this time were not so much about being thrifty and conservative but more about streamlining and creating a more elegant body shape. The severity of the economic downturn was in a shocking contrast to the wealth and excess across all aspects of society, fashion and design that was experienced in the Jazz Age. Although the general overtone of the 1920s is one of glamour and illicit indulgences, many were still living below the poverty line. Many could not afford any form of fashionable clothing – a fact often overlooked in the study of fashion history. When focusing on everyday clothing, the 1920s look was still a recognizable one; however, one must not underestimate the glaring gap between those who were able to afford

Left: Woman wearing a sophisticated mid-calf length dress with a pulled-in waist, short sleeves and a decorative pussy bow neckline detail. She wears fashionable matching gloves and hat with the ensemble, and has a matching jacket slung over her arm. (Photo: Shutterstock)

high-end fashion and those who could not. The most recognizable styles and shapes within fashion design tend to be from the higher end of fashion, which suggests it represents only a small section of society and social strata.

The transition of fashion and clothing from the 1920s to the 1930s can be illustrated by the reduction of elaborate cubist-style ornamentation and the gradual move towards a figure-hugging shape as seen in the later part of the decade and into the early 1930s. Garments were now following the natural curve of the body, clinging closely to the hips (often requiring the addition of a triangular panel inserted into the skirt at the waist) and swooping to lower hemlines. As these shapes and silhouettes were already appearing within fashion prior to the economic downturn, it is difficult to ascertain what stimulated this new direction. Typically in times of financial and economic hardships, more restrained and conservative forms of fashion dominate, particularly when considering use of fabric and the position of hemlines. In order to create a cheaper garment, less fabric is used and the hemline is predominately higher. This direction of style did not appear until later in the thirties, which many fashion historians note is an intriguing feature of the interwar years. It has also been noted by some authors that the rise in right-wing politics at the time provided an opportunity for fashion to become more conservative in its appearance. If anything, fabric usage increased in the early 1930s, given the lengthening of hemlines and the addition of small capes and other interesting accessories.

However dark and dreary the political and economic context of the 1930s was, it was also a time of modernity, glamour in fashion and streamlining in design. The era was deemed a design decade, with changes throughout the arts scene and the development of design consultancy as a profession, with the sector of consumer products on the rise. This role saw the development of more

consumer products than ever before and more avenues in which to sell them. Advancements were not restricted to just the arts sector but were evident within new technologies such as intercontinental aviation, colour photography and technicolour at the cinema.

The fashion leaders around the world embraced the new understated but elegant look of the period, with Paris maintaining its position as the epicentre of haute couture (literally, 'high fashion'); this position continues to the present day although there are now cities around the world that rival this prestigious accolade. Even in the 1930s, such cities were crucial contributors to the development of the 'modern' look that appeared during this decade of political and financial instability. This period has been referred to as the 'Golden Age of Fashion', an epoch during which a selection of industrial innovations were appropriated by leading designers and artisans. The 1930s was also a very important time for the synthesis or merging of the disciplines of art and fashion. This converging of ideas and styles had never been seen before in such an emphatic and recognizable way. The integration of art into fashion was key in the creation of a new and modern aesthetic, formally signifying the breakaway from the preceding Edwardian period that was restrictive in its social values and ideals and in its clothing.

The emblematic long and sinuous silhouette of the thirties was a very clear departure from the restrictive and, at times, oppressive modes of dress seen prior to this decade. This new silhouette gracefully accentuated the body rather than controlling it, similarly to the loosely liberating twenties-style garments. There was however, more control and focus on the female form and the celebration of it rather than merely hiding it under a shapeless tubular dress. The previously recognizable style of the 1920s flapper was a boxy chemise-style garment with a dropped waist. When considering the notoriety of the 1920s flapper dresses

and the reinvigorated fascination with Jazz Age culture, this style was surprisingly short-lived, remaining popular from about 1925 to 1928. This loose and liberating style cut all connections with the fashions of the era before WWI; however, the masking of the body and the relatively shapeless nature of the garments led to the silhouette becoming somewhat of a fashion fossil, seemingly never being embraced in full within contemporary fashion. This is in contrast to the key elements of the style associated with the 1930s, which have been recurring in fashion for more than eighty years, demonstrating its longevity and timeless aesthetic.

Styles of the 1930s

Among other features of fashion in this decade, the 1930s produced two distinct looks. The first look had an accentuated shoulder, natural waistline, fitted torso and bust, a narrow hipline and an elongated hemline. This style began to emerge in the late twenties, but was firmly in place by 1930, reflecting the new streamlined Art Moderne aesthetic that would come to dominate the decade. The woman of the thirties was a more grown-up version of the 1920s flapper girl, with a style that was described as being more 'feminine' when compared to the boyish garçonne style of the preceding decade. The new figure was slender yet curvaceous, draped in a calf-length glamorous gown with an elegantly permed bob. This new feminine silhouette involved the waistline returning to its natural position, where it remained for the rest of the decade. This waistline was more or less emphasized depending on the garment; however, it appeared more nipped in and refined from around 1933 onwards. This natural waistline was highlighted more obviously by the adoption of empire lines created by small bolero jackets, capes and the inclusion of seams just below the bust. The length of skirts was also fixed until the later years of the decade, when hemlines rose. For the majority of the thirties, calf length was used for daywear and floor length for evening dress. A slender and figure-hugging shape could be created by the insertion of a V-shaped insert, its apex just below the middle of the bustline and its sides flaring out to the hips. The skirt itself was quite often layered at the bottom, perhaps with a tiered set of ruffles or even fully pleated; in contrast, the slender and simple rolled hemline at the bottom of a plain skirt was favoured by the Art Moderne style that involved minimal ornamentation.

The torso was further accentuated by the lowering of necklines, which were decorated with ruffles, tiered collars or wide scalloped edges. There was also an appetite for trompe l'oeil effects for jumpers, for bows, ascot-style ties and corsages of fabric flowers. The back of the garment (and the wearer) was now considered to be as important as the front, with features such as plunging backlines and diamanté straps running across the back of the neck in order to highlight this. The development of back jewellery was now a common sight in high-end Hollywood-style costume, something that would soon influence trends for the average women with an interest in fashion.

By 1934, this elegant style was being supplemented by a neo-romantic element that saw hemlines rising, skirts becoming fuller and waists becoming more cinched. The 'New Look' created by Christian Dior in 1947 was inspired by many elements of the late thirties style. This suggests that WWII halted the progress of fashion design and production, and this new style was not able to flourish until the late forties rather than earlier in the decade. Given the huge economic downturn experienced during the 1930s, fewer garments were being sold and produced when compared to the influx of clothing to the market in the twenties. Regardless of the sparseness of the industry, there were still lasting innovative styles and features created at this time, which reinforces the importance of this decade in fashion history and design.

One such style was the tailored suit,

which became hugely popular in the 1930s. The practicality and versatility of the 'ensemble' of matching skirts, dresses, blouses and coats was ideal for the working woman who was rushing around town running errands and socializing. Leading designers were catering to the taste makers within society, who were expressing a taste for both elegance and ease, and the tailored suit ensemble provided them with this. The speed at which these changes within fashion were accommodated could also be attributed to the technological advances in textiles with the creation of new fibres and fabrics such as synthetic silk. The techniques of dying and printing fabrics were also greatly improving, as showcased at the Exposition Internationale des Arts Décoratifs, which was the first major international marketing platform to display new features such as this within arts and design. This event was hugely influential, with the term 'Art Deco' being coined in the 1960s in relation to the design ethos presented at this exposition. The term 'Art Deco' is often applied to all aspects of design from the 1920s through to the early 1940s; however, the term 'Art Moderne' is also used. It is important to understand the differences between these two styles and movements, as Art Deco was referred to as 'Moderne' during the twenties and was only later termed Art Deco.

It was important that everyday fashion and clothing was durable and easy to wear but also elegant and feminine. This led to fabrics such as velvet becoming hugely popular at the time, given its luxurious feel and finish. Devoré velvet was also favoured: interesting decoration could be created with this fabric patterned by the controlled burning away of the pile by an acid treatment. Cottons and linens were now also being promoted as fashionable materials, and with the use of such fabric by couturier Coco Chanel in haute couture creations in the previous decade, these fabrics were no longer associated with poverty and the working class. Their durability and

their reasonable price elevated their popularity during the 1930s, when the negative effects of the economic recession were most notably felt.

This renaissance for cheaper and more conservative fabrics did not deter

SOURCES FOR THE DECADE'S STYLE

The Art Deco style was showcased in 1925 at the Exposition Internationale des Arts Décoratifs, possibly best displayed in the context of furniture design. The style built upon the stylized and cleanly formed lines of the preceding style of Art Nouveau. There were a great number of influences on Art Deco style, such as the Greco-Roman period in which the ideals of balance and proportion were highly favoured. The Egyptian two-dimensional silhouettes found in artwork from this period and the Asian high-shine, glossy finish of lacquered artefacts can also be seen as clear influences on design for the Art Deco style. Fashion was to follow art and furniture in showing a lightness and sense of restrained ornamentation.

The Art Moderne movement developed in the USA and dates to the early 1930s. This movement shared many qualities with the Art Deco style but these were further magnified. Moderne was streamlined, and the design of furniture (for example) was considerably pared down when compared to Art Deco work. The prominence of geometric outlines was highly favoured, and there was an appreciation of the machine-made, designed to be mass-produced regardless of its mass production capabilities. Arts and design from the Moderne style displays a sense of motion in a light and uncluttered way.

the elite from opting for silks and other more expensive fabrics such as fine wool crêpes, luxurious lamés in gold and silver and silk satins. Given the advances in textile technology, it was now possible to create imitations of such fabrics successfully using man-made fibres. Fabrics like rayon or artificial silk had been developed in the previous decade; they were now gaining popularity, given the desire for skimming gowns designed to highlight and celebrate the female form. These fabrics were now rendered affordable for nearly everyone rather than merely the wealthy.

Fur capes, stoles and wraps were worn extensively for both day and night. The highest-end sable, mink, chinchilla and silver fox were all highly desirable, and the cheaper pelts such as muskrat and rabbit could be dyed to resemble nearly anything. This illustrates the desire for fur fashion in the lower end of the market too. For those who could not afford even the lower-end furs and pelts, the availability of 'processed lamb' and the wide variety of other cotton pile faux furs, demonstrates the extensive popularity of this fashion.

Ready-to-Wear and the Working Woman

Everyday fashion and clothing for the working woman had to be durable and easy to wear, but there was also a very clear desire to look elegant and on trend too. The availability of more affordable alternatives to the expensive luxury fabrics, alongside the common practice of copying haute couture designs, demonstrates a desire by women of all social classes and statuses to be fashionable and stylish. This desire was served very well by manufacturers and advertisers of fashion, who developed a very intricate retail structure that catered to society's burgeoning needs. This would become the ready-to-wear market which is considered to have led to the democratization of fashion during this era, something which now dominates in our own contemporary society.

The growth of this ready-to-wear market was also complemented by the expansion of magazine culture, which saw many lower-end publications available to assist women on the selection and purchase of fashionable ready-to-wear clothing, much in the same way that our contemporary publications provide advice, examples and suggestions on how to create or develop your own personal style. The 1930s saw ready-to-wear companies blossom, with more variety in fabric, shape and styles than ever before. This sector was additionally supported by the fast production techniques that were continually improving, and the development of catalogue companies advertising and marketing the extensive retail opportunities that were available to more women.

Catalogue shopping revolutionized the way women shopped during this decade, with companies such as Sears (in the USA) and Littlewoods (in the UK) bursting onto the scene. Catalogue retail developed in the second half of the nineteenth century, so this development was not a new one; however, given the expansion and prevalence of the railways, the consumer base was now considerably larger than the industry had previously seen. Mail order companies thrived and shopping from home was hugely convenient for the busy woman, much as it is today with the availability of online shopping. Many of these catalogue companies offered nearly everything, which removed necessity for tiresome repeat visits to the shops, especially with children in tow. The options of paying in instalments encouraged women to purchase multiple items from the one company, and the great customer service of postal discounts, hassle-free returns and a huge variety of items for sale ensured these companies built enormous loyal customer bases who greatly trusted and relied upon them.

In the UK, the company of Littlewoods distributed its first catalogue in 1932, and swiftly encouraged users to set up their own 'shilling clubs'. These clubs contained groups of women who were typically consuming or purchasing from one or more shares in the club. The money from these women was then collected up and usually amounted to a few poundsworth of goods each week. The women would then draw lots to decide the order in which they would receive their goods. All the members of the club received their goods before they had finished paying for them, except for the unlucky member who received her goods last. The organizers of these clubs tended to receive discounts on their own purchases, and the vast majority of the clubs were set up by women who would purchase fashionable clothing and accessories.

Although convenient for the club members, the clubs were a good initiative to generate and increase sales. The substantial uptake of such initiatives demonstrated the ever-increasing appetite for fashionable clothing by all classes and social strata. The range of products available also expanded significantly during the 1930s, as there was a desire to wear fashionable garments that were clearly inspired by the luxurious evening wear of haute couture houses. There was also an increase in the purchasing of fashionable but functional daywear ranges for the average working woman. The variety of clothing available from companies such as Littlewoods and Sears illustrates the growing diversity in leisure activities and pastime destinations now available to nearly all of society. It was no longer just the social elite who could afford to wear luxurious-looking evening wear to an event, but those of more conservative means too.

Influence of Paris and the Semi-Made Revolution

The 1930s saw the expansion of fashion catalogues and ready-to-wear companies offering copies of high-end fashion garments. The role of the haute couture industry of Paris in the twenties and thirties, as in many other decades of fashion, was that of sole and undisputed dictator of taste, elegance and luxurious women's clothing. The Paris houses were looked upon to set the tone for future styles and trends, and the world would follow. Although other major cities such as London and New York had hugely successful fashion industries, it was felt the capital of Fashion would always be Paris (an accolade this city has continued to maintain in the eyes of many). During the 1920s, consumers of fashion from all over the globe would congregate on Paris twice a year to purchase the latest designs from their personally favoured couturiers.

It was not just individual customers who would undertake this pilgrimage to Paris, but the department stores, catalogue companies and ready-to-wear manufacturers would also travel from far and wide to report back on the trends their customers would expect to see after being showcased in Paris. Copying or interpreting has long since been a crucial feature of the dissemination of fashion. There was an awareness of this, which led to couturiers offering official duplication garments both to capitalize on this external market and to regulate the level of imitation. These designer-branded models were leased to ready-to-wear manufacturers and retailers who could then copy the garments exactly and retail them under the couturier's name in large department stores, making high-end fashion available to a broader market. Toiles were also sold for similar purposes to the middle market – retailers and manufacturers – with the couture house even offering paper patterns for the lower end of the market. This ensured that the seasonal stylistic changes and features of Parisian fashion were filtered down throughout the industry to the rest of the world in a controlled and measured way.

This system of copying was dramatically shaken after the 1929 Wall Street Crash. Americans were encouraged to 'buy local' during this period of economic instability, through heavily patriotic advertising campaigns in which fashion journalists and socialites endorsed American fashion.

In order to emphasize the importance of buying local whilst undermining the consumption of foreign goods, there was a huge increase in import taxes. For Paris this was as high as 90 per cent, which could easily have destroyed their fashion market, as American money was one of their largest streams of income.

One of the ways in which American purchasers of Parisian fashion would navigate and ultimately avoid paying these extremely high import taxes was by cutting the couture labels out of the garments. This would explain why there are so many items of couture-made Parisian garments within museum collections that are currently unidentified due to their lack of label. Although these types of tax hikes made it more difficult to consume Parisian clothing, purchasing did not cease altogether as the world relied very heavily on Paris to set the tone for all things chic. It was not just the individual clientele who reduced their purchasing, but large department stores had to purchase more wisely, thus restricting what was now available. It was not uncommon for department stores to club together and buy a collection of designs or styles; however, some stopped completely and relied solely on the production of copies.

In response to this changing dynamic, couturiers started slashing the prices of garments by up to half, which was only feasible by creating simpler, less fussy designs that required less labour and fabric. Another way in which the Parisian haute couture market tempted customers was through the availability of semi-couture creations that only required one or two fittings. This was considerably cheaper than a traditional couture garment, and the option to purchase a lower-cost, less intricate, limited-edition garment was offered by many of the couture houses. Some designers utilized cheaper man-made fabrics more readily in their clothing, some increased their ready-to-wear range, and some even started to offer mail order.

The desire to purchase investment pieces led to the slowing of changes in styles, as there was an appetite for elegant classics rather than the latest trend. It was a difficult time for couture houses and some ended up closing in response to slowing sales. In order to survive, many houses turned to accessories and perfumes, and the expansion of this market ensured the survival of the industry as a whole. The ready-to-wear market developed swiftly, offering a much wider range of well-made and affordable fashion. The changes in the post-Great War silhouette, which ultimately simplified clothing, made copying of high-end designs much easier to do; however, it was the perfectly fitting garment that remained the distinction of the wealthy clients of couture houses from those buying ready-to-wear. Sizes varied dramatically on the ready-to-wear market as there was no existing standardized sizing data; each company had its own set of sizes which rendered it difficult to secure a perfect fit from different suppliers. The previous loose-fitting tubular dresses of the 1920s did not rely on precise sizing given the style and cut of the garments, but the figure-hugging fluid garments of the 1930s required an exact size.

Sears offered semi-made garments that were delivered partially complete with just simple seams and finishing to be undertaken by the customer, allowing for personal adjustments which made for very well-fitting clothing. The offer of semi-made ensembles was in response to the desire for well-fitting fashionable clothes, and to combat the ongoing issues associated with a lack of standardized sizing. It also allowed for more women to have access to fashionable and well-fitting affordable clothing after the economic downturn. Many of the clients of couture houses could no longer afford the luxury of made-to-measure clothing, which boosted the sales of semi-made garments, ensuring customers could wear well-made and well-fitting clothing for a fraction of the cost. Companies such as Sears had to

Woman wearing a silk floor-length gown with mid-length puffed sleeves and a small collar. Hanging from her collar are tassels with decorative piped pom-poms on the end. (Photo: Shutterstock)

reassure the customers these semi-made ensembles could be completed by even the most inexperienced of makers. Promotional material using this angle suggests the companies were aware that the new customers purchasing these semi-made ensembles were previously clients of couturiers, for whom it was not necessary to be equipped with practical sewing skills in the same way it would have been for the working class.

Wealthy former clients of couturiers had to limit their expenditure on clothing, and in some cases even find employment. This made the convenience of catalogue shopping or ordering semi-made ensembles even more appealing, which itself contributed to the broadening of the variety and range of clothing styles available within this section of the fashion industry. For the working-class women who could not afford to buy any form of fashionable clothing, home dressmaking remained a popular choice. This method allowed those who were keen to wear fashionable clothing and maintain a sense of style to do so on a very tight budget. This encouraged pattern companies to offer an ever-growing variety of patterns to produce fashion-focused clothing at home. Many of these pattern companies formed partnerships with well-known Parisian couture houses, thus adding an element of glamour and exclusivity to the garments you could create. This demonstrates the continuing role Paris played in setting the tone for on-trend fashion.

Classicism

The major artistic movements of Abstraction and Surrealism were very important in the inspiration of fashion design within the 1930s; however, classicism and its revival developed one of the quintessential looks of this decade. This movement spearheaded the streamlined Grecian aesthetic that the thirties can be characterized by, with an emphasis being placed on the natural body, one that could be easily distinguished in the satin figure-

hugging gowns that were dominating. Although the thirties decade was strongly focused on the emancipation of women, the female form and modernism, this very historic revival would dominate inspiration for some time, demonstrating the foundation that the Greco-Roman period built, on which the Art Moderne aesthetic could develop.

The best examples of classically inspired design were beautiful to look at as well as being highly functional. This movement reflected the ideals of the greatest advocate of this style, couturier Madeleine Vionnet. Paris was still the artistic centre of Europe in the early part of the twentieth century, and the progressive artistic and design movement of Art Nouveau was dominant within the arts and architecture. Madeleine Vionnet was determined to eliminate the corset whilst also creating a new style of clothing that freed the female form from the restraints of this undergarment. Vionnet was passionate about creating a fluid garment unbound from restraints, allowing the wearer to move freely without wearing a corset of any kind. This new spirit, or Spirit Nouveau as it was called, aligned with the other aesthetic revolutionaries of the early twentieth century such as dancer Isadora Duncan and architect Le Corbusier.

The collective revival of classicism gathered momentum during and after WWI and greatly affected many of the avant-garde artists of the time, even 'causing them to modify the revolutionary styles they themselves had invented', as Cowling and Mundy put it. This revival inspired all areas of the arts, including sculpture, architecture and, importantly, fashion. It was the cornerstone of the Art Moderne aesthetic. It was not just the major designers and couturiers who found inspiration in the Art Moderne aesthetic, but also fashion photographers such as George Hoyningen-Huene and Horst P. Horst. The way in which Huene placed the model and utilized lighting and space captured the classically inspired

perfection of couture garments.

Paris laid claim to being the most trailblazing, trend-setting and innovative force in Western fashion design long before the 1930s. Despite this, even with clothing being designed and made, and ultimately being shipped all around the globe (thus inspiring other makers), Paris still struggled during the Great Depression especially when considering their most lucrative years had been in the 1920s. It was not all success and glamour in Paris at this time, with a number of couture houses consolidating or even closing down due to poor sales. The leading firms were producing around half the number of garments turned out in the 1920s, and the huge advertising campaigns that were seen in America all but ceased in the thirties. Companies that worked on intricate detailing such as beading and embroidery were impacted the most during the downturn of the economy. The simplifying of styles and the minimalist aesthetic that was becoming hugely popular rendered surface decoration obsolete, and the companies that specialized in this, near obsolete too.

Women were dominating the modern fashion industry in Paris until WWII, a phenomenon that had never been seen before. The appearance of nearly four dozen couture houses within the major editorial and advertising spaces of Vogue and Harper's Bazaar in the 1930s included designers such as Lanvin, Chanel and Schiaparelli. Even the lesser-known designers such as Ana de Pambo (for Paquin) and Nina Ricci found a place within these publications. This dominance of female couturiers in France during these interwar years is attributed to a number of reasons, one of them being the severe loss of men during WWI. France's low birth rate and the rise of the feminist movement also encouraged more women to take up work outside the home. Women were moving to the forefront of fashion; this change, along with the clothing they developed, produced an impact that has lasted ever since.

Sewing to create clothing had been largely a traditionally feminine industry. However, the late eighteenth and nineteenth centuries saw major changes; as in other industries, there was specialization, mechanization and managerial development. At the top of the industry, making clothing became couture. The couture industry was transformed from a mere craft into a high art and a very lucrative business by male couturiers such as Charles Frederick Worth. It was a widely held belief at the time that men were more naturally gifted with artistic talent, and women were thought to be just the technical labourers. The skill involved in turning these designs created by the male 'genius' into real garments was considered mundane and involving limited creativity. The idea that a technician or a dressmaker could also be a great artist or designer was simply unthinkable at this time, and unfortunately the term 'dressmaker' still has negative connotations today. It was not until the 1920s and 1930s that couturiers such as Vionnet brought the craft of dressmaking and technical skill to the creative design process.

When Madeleine Vionnet opened her own fashion house, female couturiers were beginning to compete successfully with their male counterparts. It was designers such as Vionnet and Coco Chanel who were consolidating the work of the pioneers before them in the preceding generation, such as Madame Jeanne Paquin in the first ten years of the twentieth century. Paquin not only had a couture house that employed over 1,000 workers, but was regarded as one of the world's leading fashion authorities. The lack of fame for Paquin today is due to her male competitor Paul Poiret, who has received more attention in the study of historical fashion. Paquin made her garments from the finest fabrics with detailing and surface decoration undertaken very precisely and to extremely high standards, whereas Poiret made dramatic and memorable garments that were inconsistent in their quality and execution. Given the role of men in society at this time and similarly today, the female designer was overshadowed by her male counterpart.

Vionnet and the Bias Cut

One of the most notable design features of fashion in the 1930s was the use of the bias cut most conspicuously popularized by the designer Madeleine Vionnet. The bias cut was achieved by cutting fabric at a 45-degree angle rather than on the warp or the weft. The bias cut allowed for designers to create sculptural gowns that would closely hug the figure, by essentially draping or manipulating the fabric around the different contours of the body. Vionnet rejected everything that distracted from or distorted the natural curves of the body. Taking inspiration from the avant-garde dancer Isadora Duncan, Vionnet designed and created garments that floated around the body freely, demonstrating her understanding that fabrics cut on the bias could be draped in sinuous folds to highlight and complement the fluidity of the female form.

Vionnet favoured silks, satins and crêpe de chine for creating a luxurious and elegant silhouette, both sensual and modern, that created the quintessential look of the 1930s. She is considered by some as the greatest couturier of the twentieth century, given her ability to drape on the dressmaking stand. Madeleine began her career as a dressmaker at the very young age of eleven, working excessively long hours like many other girls at this time. Born in Paris, Vionnet worked in England for five years before returning to Paris where she secured a position with the highly respected couture house of Callot Soeurs – the Callot Sisters. Vionnet's talents were swiftly recognized by the chief designer Madame Marie Callot Gerber, and she was given the position of head of the workrooms. The sisters relied solely on Vionnet to transform their ideas into working toiles and ultimately into garments. This provided the couturier with a great deal of experience, something she commented on when recalling her days at Callot Soeurs. This experience elevated her knowledge and understanding for fabric and the ways in which it could be manipulated. It also gave her a greater understanding and appreciation of craftsmanship and creation, providing her with a solid foundation from which she could develop and progress within the world of haute couture. Vionnet first opened her own couture fashion house in 1912; however, this was very short-lived and she went out of business at the onset of WWI. Leaving Paris to live in Rome for the duration of the war, Vionnet then returned to open what became one of the most successful couture houses of the time, producing from 1918 to 1939. At the peak of the business, she was employing over 1,200 workers, and was a notoriously generous and loyal employer, demonstrating an appreciation for all of her workers and their skills.

During the last years of her career, Vionnet fully realized her artistic vision of removing restrictions and encumbrances such as corsetry from women's fashion. This rendered her one of the most trailblazing couturiers as she disrupted the basic construction of European fashion which had, until then, remained relatively unchanged for several hundred years. Whilst most notable for exploiting cutting fabric on the bias, Vionnet also married both art and fashion into one aesthetic vision, something her peer Elsa Schiaparelli would take even further. In order to avoid the age-old problem of bias-draped fabric being stretched out of shape, Vionnet managed to tame the wild and unwieldy nature of the bias by sewing together two pattern pieces which were cut on the straight grain along two diagonal lines. This allowed her to create a body-skimming tube that would slip easily over the head and cling to the figure. The elegant and soft draping nature of her designs was further enhanced due to her avoidance of darts, waistbands and inner linings.

Vionnet insisted on eliminating rigid under-layers or restrictive underwear, and is considered by many to be a pioneering force in the liberation of women and the progression of modern dressing. Vionnet's philosophy and approach to design can be illustrated by her views on undergarments: she was famously quoted as saying, 'A woman's muscles are the best corset one could imagine'. Although very liberating, the clothing she created would become high fashion and would also require the wearer to have an ideal body, given the skimming nature of these fluid gowns. Although most of Vionnet's gowns were unadorned, highlighting the simplicity of the fabric and the shapely figure beneath, she did occasionally opt for subtle forms of decoration. One such approach was to manipulate the surface of the ground fabric through tiny hand-sewn pin-tucks, creating the illusion of fine and delicate decoration, almost imperceptible to the eye when standing back from the gown.

Using quadrants was a clever innovation by Vionnet that evolved due to the couturier draping all her designs on the stand; she developed this very precise form of construction in order to create more coherent garments. She produced her most successful work when combining the precision of geometry with the sensual drama of a full-skirted silhouette. Such handiwork was standard for Vionnet, as demonstrated by the interiors of her garments that were hand-finished to the highest sewing standards. Unlike other couture houses, Vionnet's overcast stitches were so small and perfectly placed that they appeared to have been sewn on a machine, a skill many admired and attempted to emulate. The seam allowances on her gowns were also very small, similar to those on lingerie, in order to ensure an unbroken line. The hems were very tightly rolled and finished in the same way as a handkerchief. A very common issue experienced by couturiers who utilized the bias-cut technique was that it was very unwieldy and the hemlines

often fell out or down. Vionnet avoided this, creating tight and secure hemlines, a mystery to some. The hemlines on a Vionnet dress were notoriously secure, because all the garments would be weighted and stretched out after being cut in the Vionnet workrooms, sometimes for a number of weeks, before the hem was eventually re-cut, rolled and stitched. This was a long and painstaking process, one you would rarely find in fashion production today.

Lanvin

Another of the female couturiers in Paris working in the 1930s was Jeanne Lanvin, considered one of the greatest couturiers of the twentieth century. She began her career in fashion working as a delivery girl for the milliner Suzanne Talbot in 1880, but went on to open her own millinery shop within the decade and then branched out into clothing by 1909. It was after WWI that Lanvin would be running the most significant houses of couture in the world. This empire would soon expand to include a men's tailoring atelier and an activewear shop. For some, Lanvin was considered relatively unglamorous as a person and dresser, which some authors have suggested may account for her relatively limited coverage when compared to innately chic and stylish couturiers such as Coco Chanel. Lanvin's creations were also fairly archetypal in their feminine appearance, which did not fit well with the masculine garçonne style of the 1920s and later the Moderne aesthetic of the thirties. Extremely skilled in surface ornamentation, Lanvin opted for very intricate and skilled decoration such as embroidery; however, like other leading couturiers she altered her style from this intricate and fine surface decoration on soft and billowing robes de style, and moved towards creating slender sheath dresses that highlighted fabric contrasts and architectural patterns.

Chanel

As compared to Jeanne Lanvin, who lived a relatively quiet life out of the spotlight, Gabrielle 'Coco' Chanel was a celebrity. She would go on to become the most notable fashion designer in the world, still to this day remembered as one of the greatest in fashion history. Although hugely important at the time, she was in no way the dominant couturier of the 1930s, and started her business under the financial support of her two lovers. Unlike some of the other designers of the time who worked their way from the bottom up, Chanel spent time as a rather scandalous café singer, and as a kept woman to wealthy men. Chanel's style was edgy, and she created her own looks based on men's attire. Although she was not the first female to be wearing masculine clothing, Chanel wore it in a different way: she created a male look but essentially made it feminine, a style of dressing that is hugely popular today. Chanel has consistently been awarded accolades incorrectly, such as creating the little black dress; however, her early activewear designs were truly innovative even though she was not the first to have created such garments. Rather than a solo visionary, Chanel was hugely skilled in utilizing, adapting and publicizing looks that were created by others. There was something so intriguing and interesting about her way that she elevated herself to the top of the fashion industry by embracing and developing her skills as a very fashionable and innovative stylist.

Schiaparelli

Elsa Schiaparelli is most known for her Surrealist-inspired design from the mid to late 1930s, leading to her becoming one of the most influential designers in twentieth-century fashion. She was one of the first couturiers to integrate complex artistic concepts into highly functional and wearable garments. A great deal has been written about Schiaparelli and her foray into the world of art, in particular her connections to Surrealism. Given the emphasis that has been placed on this side of her artistic output, her skills or lack of skills in fashion design and making have been in question over the years. Elsa tended to apply two-dimensional shapes and images onto structured and tailored suits, utilizing another organization to undertake the embroidery involved, and she avoided innovative cutting techniques; however, she did often choose to work with fabric in an organic way similar to a sculptor. Given her affinity with sculpture, she worked with fabric as her medium and considered fashion an art form, moulding shapes and draping fabrics on live models using the fabric she intended for the final garment. This was not a standard way of working, and a toile would normally be created before the final fabric would be cut or utilized.

Schiaparelli created surrealist designs using techniques other than just embroidery and button placement. She employed textile firms to create transparent and reflective fabrics, also materials that mimicked tree bark, in order to create garments that were visual expressions of complex ideas such as self-reflection, invisibility and the illusion of placement and displacement of elements from nature. Schiaparelli also fully embraced the Art Moderne aesthetic and is credited with popularizing the sharply angular suit which would dominate fashion in the late 1930s. She further enhanced this modern aesthetic by only wearing black or white: this reductive dressing was chic, modern and also highly functional in a time of great economic crisis.

Hollywood Glamour

As well as being a fruitful era for fashion and art, it was undisputedly the 'Golden Age' of Hollywood, with dozens of films being produced each week to appeal to a mass audience in the USA. It was no longer just trends in hair and make-up that were heavily influenced by what the stars of the Hollywood film industry were doing, but it was fashion too. Women started

to look to Hollywood for their fashion inspiration. The elite haute couture market was not enthused by Hollywood costumes as they were deemed vulgar and too populist, and fashionable clothing was much too understated for the screen. However, for the everyday woman who could not afford to use a couturier, the silver screen was the place to source ideas and inspiration.

After some time, the elite couturiers of Paris could no longer ignore the impact Hollywood was having on the fashion industry, and began to understand how they could use it to their advantage. There were several memorable fashions launched by Hollywood. As movies could take up to a year to be completed and released, the costumiers working on these films realized if the clothes were modelled too closely on the latest Parisian fashions they would date much too quickly. In order to avoid this the costumiers would produce original designs for each film. These designs tended to echo the styles of the thirties Parisian silhouette, but the detailing was significantly different. Detailing of the silver screen was in no way discreet. The elegance and chicness of the 1930s was ramped up to excessive glamour in Hollywood through ornamentation and excessive surface decoration.

Whilst film costume designers took inspiration from fashion around them, they were also credited with having started or inspired trends of their own. The revival of historicism and neo-romanticism in fashion could be attributed to the Hollywood industry, with notable couturiers such Elsa Schiaparelli following suit and creating collections inspired by specific looks from within certain films.

Hollywood associated itself with spectacular high fashion, with the some of its notable creators starting their careers in the rag trade: Samuel Goldwyn was a glove salesman, William Fox inspected fabrics for garment traders, and Henry Warner worked in the shoe repair business. Given their backgrounds, all of the major film-makers of the time appreciated the power of fashion and

could clearly see the marketing opportunities tied up within it.

There were two very clear strategies of consumption that were actively encouraged by the industry. One strategy was to employ costume designers who used the latest trends as their source of inspiration to create stylish films for the fashion-conscious audience. The star-studded events to showcase these films provided a platform for these fashionable creations to spread all round the USA, broadening the reach of fashionable clothing even further. Both film studios and the costume designers they employed capitalized on the popularity of their garments. Licensed copies soon appeared in shops, and influential clothing companies struck deals with the film studios to sell copies.

In order to take this concept even further, Bernard Waldman established the Modern Merchandizing Bureau in 1930, which supplied exclusive reproductions of film fashions to more than 1,400 shops across America. In-house 'cinema shops' in retailers such as Macy's were advertised in movie magazines to assist women in locating their nearest outlet. These publications tempted women to buy the magazine by using fashion competitions in which a lucky reader could win a copy of her favourite starlet's dress. These campaigns both generated magazine sales and also enhanced the appetite for Hollywood-inspired garments from well-known films. Even those who could not afford ready-to-wear clothing were not excluded, as many of these publications included vouchers in the back of the magazine that allowed home dressmakers to order patterns taken from the onscreen outfits, once again ensuring that fashion really was for all.

The second strategy was to showcase commodities and to create partnerships with brand name manufacturers. Movie moguls were subjected to a level of pressure by various successful brands and corporations to produce modern movies with modern products making an appearance. This strategy revolved around a contractual agreement

Portrait of Amelia Earhart (1897–1937), 1932 by E.F. Foley. Earhart is wearing a lace bias-cut full-length dress with matching jacket and decorative waist belt. This photo highlights the focus on surface pattern and detailing of fabric. (Photo: Shutterstock)

between the studio and the brand, which would ensure the film featured some form of product placement. The earliest example of this product placement was a popular branded drink appearing on screen; however, there were also many opportunities for objects that were more in keeping with the film and that blended in more naturally.

Modern goods such as cars, clothes, fridges and varied household goods were all utilized to generate sales. The film studios even hired dedicated staff within their own exploitation department to break down the film into a list of the possible objects that might make an appearance, and then seek any potential product sponsors. As one might imagine, this way of working greatly influenced the scripting of films, with the potential for sponsorship always in mind; this unquestionably shaped consumer choice within fashion and other commodities. As well as boosting the budget of films, the onscreen stars also cashed in on this lucrative relationship. Stars were awarded licences to put their names to products so fans or children could own a piece of their favourite star. These goods, usually hair accessories, toys and household items, became hugely collectable, as did the postcards that normally accompanied them. These cards were similar to a Pokémon card, with information about the star – their fashion favourites, style choices and so on.

The films were complemented by large-scale promotional campaigns that were sponsored by the brand manufacturers whose products had been incorporated into the film. These advertisements were huge and allowed the branded manufacturer to generate huge sales whilst the film studios could also ensure the film reached a mass audience. The brands were then able to utilize the onscreen stars in their own product campaigns, demonstrating the hugely beneficial impact these partnerships had on everyone involved.

Fashion in Germany

Like so many other countries, Germany had followed the fashions coming out of Paris; however, given the huge upheaval and impeding tragedy that was bubbling under the surface in 1930s Germany, this would not last for ever. When Adolf Hitler came to power, he was keen to distance Germany from anything and anyone that did not represent his Aryan 'ideal'. One of the ways in which he did this was by setting up the 'Association of German Aryan Manufacturers' in 1933. This was to ensure the Aryanization of the fashion industry within Germany. This association would showcase the latest German fashion collections being created, normally the week before Paris Fashion Week, in a bid to reinforce the originality and authenticity of German design. The Nazi party ensured Germany distanced itself from all 'foreign degenerate' influences, pitching itself as the most innovative power in fashion design. In the same way that British wartime utility clothing scheme garments were labelled with CC41 labels, the ADEFA label was applied to all garments from makers approved by the association. These labels were used to assure the wearer that only suitable 'Aryan hands' had made this piece of clothing.

Like many of the abhorrent views that Adolf Hitler possessed, he considered the haute couture fashion industry as a manifestation of the 'Jewish Conspiracy'. This led to women in Germany being actively discouraged from wearing items of clothing made or inspired by other countries, as he considered this to be un-German. There was even a list of such items to avoid provided by the Nazis, and a list of alternative ways in which women could dress in order to avoid embracing these foreign looks and ultimately values. The traditional German clothing, or Trachten, was promoted to be a suitable expression of the correct spiritual demeanour and solid unity of the rural community. This form of dress was not embraced by huge numbers, as one might imagine; however, German fashions do show many traditional influences. Part of this spiritual demeanour was the pursuit of health and fitness which was encouraged by other countries too. The 1920s saw the popularization of health and fitness, and the importance of these pursuits grew in the 1930s.

Activewear

Activewear garments remained popular for daywear as the comfort that was offered by this style of clothing suited the modern liberated woman's lifestyle. Changes in activewear paralleled the innovations in both men's and women's everyday clothing, and the boom in sporting activities and events during the thirties required greatly improved activewear for both the participant of the sport and the attendee. People also had more time to spare, with a shortened working week which allowed them to both enjoy and participate in more sporting activities and events. The Great Depression also increased the attendance to sporting events, as people needed a way to temporarily escape the woes associated with such an economic downturn. This was made possible by ticket prices being reduced with the aim of filling stadiums. There were also a number of new pools and tennis courts built for people to enjoy, and there were now more opportunities to travel for those wealthy few who were not affected by the economic crisis. Luxury resort destinations such as California and Palm Beach were now more accessible than ever with regular commercial air travel. This resulted in the birth of resort wear for holidays and summering in beautiful destinations, or to be worn on cruise ships such as the Queen Mary whose maiden voyage was in 1936, or the Normandie in 1932.

Fabric developments revolutionized activewear, and designers began streamlining garments to reduce bulk to allow for more freedom of movement for the wearer. The role of activewear increased in the 1930s, given the changes to the fashionable silhouette. This shift in silhouette saw a rise in women playing sports in order to perfect their figures, which were now more visible than ever before. The liberation of the figure had begun in the previous decade, when unfitted tubular dresses were favoured over corseted ensembles; however, although the looser-fitting dress was more freeing than garments from earlier decades, the wearing of a tight-fitting girdle was still necessary in order to create a tubular shape beneath the dress.

As the 1930s silhouette appeared, it became clear that undergarments were no longer deemed necessary when wearing a figure-hugging bias-cut gown. This silhouette and the revival in classicism brought with it the need to have a near-perfect figure without the use of shaping undergarments such as corsets. This Greek-style silhouette emphasized the breasts of the female form, with slight curves of the body being accentuated. Exercise was mainly promoted as a means to achieve this desired figure, and the liberated woman also had more time to enjoy sports. Women now had access to appropriate loosely fitting activewear to undertake these sports.

Some designers embraced this new lifestyle as a source of inspiration. One such was Jean Patou who felt compelled to embrace this new active lifestyle, debuting his first sport collection in the summer of 1922. Patou was an athlete himself and understood the need for an appropriate activewear garment. By closely observing sports, Patou embedded construction details into his designs in order to aid the wearer's performance. He even went on to open a sports boutique within his couture house that had sections dedicated to different sports. Each section was elaborately decorated with a background display, and there were large props to aid fitting, such as a full-size horse on which women could sit and test the fit of their riding breeches.

Patou's relationship with other athletes ensured that he based his designs on experience and understanding of how the body moved and functioned. His brother-in-law was a French national tennis player; this provided Patou with many contacts, one of the most important in his network

being tennis star Suzanne Lenglen. In 1921, Lenglen shocked the crowds of Wimbledon when she sported her custom tennis outfit designed by Patou. This ensemble included a white pleated knee-length skirt, a sleeveless white cardigan and a bright orange headband. The skirt length was considered horrifying and socially unacceptable at this time, and it was not until 1924 that skirts across all sections of fashion rose to the knee. The lack of hat in favour of a headband, along with the exposing of her arms, was considered hugely radical. As time moved on, it became more acceptable to expose your arms and lower legs, and it was considered innovative and groundbreaking to create such a wearable tennis outfit.

Whilst the female athletes of the day pushed boundaries with daring and innovative outfits that progressed social acceptability for women, men were wearing equally progressive ensembles too. In 1927 René Lacoste debuted his famed white fitted polo shirt with an embroidered crocodile logo on the chest and soon after this debut he collaborated with the French hosiery manufacturer André Gillier to mass-produce it. This would go on to influence many other fashion manufacturers to reproduce versions of the polo for various different price points during the 1930s.

Resort Wear

Resort wear began emerging as early at 1913 when Chanel opened her first boutique in the luxury resort of Deauville in north-west France. Clients could buy ready-to-wear pieces that were suitable for wearing on the beach, and garments made from jersey. It would soon become clear there was a very strong market attached to resort destinations, which led her to open a second boutique in Biarritz in south-west France. Holidaying underwent quite a transformation in the 1920s, and this cultural shift saw people now spending much of their summer at the beach rather than taking time off during the winter. It was now popular

to have a suntan which denoted having a healthy body; this was quite the opposite to the desire for pale skin in the previous years.

The development of the 'resort' happened gradually but was greatly encouraged by the activities of Sara and Gerald Murphy, wealthy American expatriates. They took the novel step of persuading the Hotel de Cap in Antibes to remain open during the summer for them to entertain their friends, who included Pablo Picasso, F. Scott Fitzgerald and Ernest Hemingway. As time passed it became more and more common for hotels to stay open during the summers to entertain guests, who of course displayed the latest fashions. The popularization of sunbathing and swimming and the influx of wealthy entrepreneurial people led to quiet fishing villages becoming luxury resorts.

During this time ocean voyaging on new luxury cruise ships was fast becoming the new way to travel. Fashion and etiquette at sea were more relaxed than on land, which led to more relaxed clothing worn on deck. For example, beach pyjamas became a very popular garment of choice to wear on board. These tended to be one-piece jumpsuits, often in bold colours and prints, with an open back and a wide-leg trouser. On land and outside of this casual environment, trousers were still deemed unacceptable for women.

Although more progressive in many areas of fashion, 1920s swimwear still came with many rules and regulations associated with the exposure of the skin. It was common for police to patrol the beaches in America, measuring bathing suits to ensure they were no shorter than six inches above the knee.

Swimwear

The development of public swimming pools democratized the activity of swimming and provided more opportunities to flaunt and showcase the latest swimsuit styles. This platform allowed for photographers of the time, such as Huene, to capture sunbathers

Woman wearing bias-cut jumpsuit with a sophisticated and sensual low-cut back. This example of resort wear demonstrates the more relaxed nature of clothing on board ships, in which women were wearing more revealing garments. (Photo: Shutterstock)

of the modern era and the new swimsuit designs that would shortly follow. One of the largest swimwear manufacturers of the time was the Oregon-based company Jantzen, who branded all their garments with the iconic diving girl logo. Other competitors included Catalina and Cole of California who were both based in Los Angeles and would dominate in the swimwear market, both in the USA and in the UK.

The 1930s saw a huge fabric revolution, with many new fibres bursting onto the market with stretchy, shiny and water-resistant qualities. For those who could afford it, that was the end of the knitted bathing suit, although many women continued to knit their own. In 1931 the Dunlop Rubber Company made a leap forward when they produced Lastex, a very fine elastic yarn made from latex rubber wrapped in cotton, rayon or (eventually) nylon. With its stretchy qualities, this fibre could be woven into different types of fabrics and incorporated into knitted bathing suits which would revolutionize the fit. This left behind the woollen bathing suit, which absorbed water, losing its shape and fit and becoming very saggy and cumbersome. Lastex, 'the miracle yarn' as it would be advertised, eliminated this issue and soon companies such as Jantzen and BVD had produced their own version of the wonder fabric.

Lastex worked particularly well with artificial fibres, allowing for a broader spectrum of colours and prints. It also allowed bathing suits to mould to the body like a second skin, unlike traditional knitted swimsuits that flattened the chest in a straight line from breastbone to waist, sagging uncontrollably and unflatteringly when wet. The incredible shaping power of Lastex led to a new way of thinking about the body. Every dimple, curve or bump was visible in a Lastex maillot: this once again prompted new ways of suppressing defects, smoothing over bulges and enhancing strengths. The construction of swimsuits became more sophisticated in the 1930s, with intricate supportive elements and darts incorporated to create a shapelier silhouette.

Structuring devices were created to flatten the tummy and narrow the waist while highlighting the bosom. BVD were the first to incorporate inbuilt bras in their swimsuits, while the important 'floating bra' designed by Gantner & Mattern could now be detached from the outer layer. Jantzen introduced its 'moulded fit' which was designed to accentuate the bustline using a series of darts and BVD also created the 'seamless side' suit which smoothed out any bulges or bumps along the waistline.

The term 'maillot' described the tight-fitting one-piece bathing suit of the 1920s that consisted of a tank-style top, high-cut legs and a low neckline. As a slimline suit, this style was unforgiving to the less-than-perfect figure. As the years progressed, the 'dressmaker' style became very popular as it was more sympathetic to the body-conscious wearer, with its tummy

A woman standing by a swimming pool in an elegant woollen bathing suit with belted waist and matching cap. (Photo: Shutterstock)

ruffles, mini-skirts and fabric aprons that could conceal lumps and bumps. Achieving the perfect tan was the goal for most sunbathers at this time, and swimsuit manufacturers designed suits to accommodate this. The 'Shouldaire' swimsuits created by Jantzen in 1931 had a drawstring above the bust and around the neck that allowed sunbathers to lower the straps of their suits in order to achieve a strap-free tan. The crab-back bathing suit was also debuted in 1931, becoming hugely popular with both men and women: the cut-outs at the back mimicked the outline of a crab, hence the name. This style, like many others at the time, was designed to provide the wearer with greater sun exposure whilst still ensuring that standards of decency were met.

In the UK, less sunshine and limited beach life meant the British swimwear market was conservative. Knitted swimsuits stayed popular for much longer and small salaries meant that Hollywood glamour-inspired Lastex suits were out of reach for most people. By the end of the 1930s, more affordable versions of the fibre were produced which saw Lastex bathing suits replace woollen ones. In spite of its shaping capabilities, designers were looking for alternative solutions to Lastex as the rubber tended to crack and perish quickly. In 1938, DuPont introduced the first version of nylon. This was a hugely popular fabric but would soon be removed from the fashion market in order to make parachutes and uniforms during the war.

The rise of activewear in the 1930s had a huge impact on issues of morality, social standards and body image. The function and ease of activewear paved the way for sportswear. Streamlining forms and ensuring the body was liberated allowed men to play sports with greater movement, and women to participate at a competitive level with men. This new silhouette and the unrestrained nature of the garments signalled a physical and psychological emancipation for women, allowing them to move, stretch and bend with minimal restrictions. The exposure of skin in the sun challenged levels of morality for both men and women, which greatly expanded society's tolerance of and embracement of activewear.

Accessories, Hair and Make-Up

Handmade garments could be accessorized with cheaper but glamorous-looking ready-made accessories such as diamanté dress clips, necklaces, bracelets, brooches, faux fur handbags and a variety of shoes. Among the most important accessories for a fashionable woman of the 1930s were gloves, with elbow-length versions for evening wear, and short or 'opera' length for daywear. This desire for glamorous accessories was picked up by retailers who introduced matching accessory ensembles such as hats, gloves, shoes and bags in a range of striking colours. Shoes were now available in a huge range of styles – flats, pumps, lace-ups, ankle-strap and buckled. The appearance of low-heeled two-tone brogues are a recognizable accessory of the early thirties, in both men and women's fashion. Handbags changed very little when compared to those of the previous decade, with beaded bags and mesh enamelled bags being popular choices during the early thirties; however, as the decade progressed leather bags became increasingly popular. Hats remained an essential element for any daytime look, with most fashionable women considering it simply vulgar to leave the house with an unadorned head. In terms of style, hats became more elegant and feminine in their shape, similar to the 1930s silhouette. Rather than wearing head-covering cloche hats as had been so popular in the twenties, smaller more delicate skullcaps and berets were the headgear of choice. This was in addition to the new fashion for large-brimmed straw hats.

Changes to hair styles during the 1930s saw a fuller more glamorous hairdo, when compared to the tight-sculpted 1920s bob. This bob was replaced with a more voluminous demi-wave or finger-waved perm: this change in hair style is connected to developments in the technicalities of hair dressing. Although earlier versions of the heated roller machine had appeared, it was not until the 1930s that the perming process became much safer. Similar to dying hair, perming required chemicals and so it was not until the thirties, when knowledge about these chemicals enabled their safe use, that perming became more popular.

Given the developments in the knowledge of hair dying, there was a shift in taste to peroxide blonde hair. The popularity for bleached hair came about in response to the trends developing in Hollywood which would start to influence the world. Similarly, Hollywood had been responsible for influencing the previous decade in its popularization of visible make-up. This influence continued into the 1930s, when Max Factor started selling cosmetics to the mainstream market rather than just within the film industry. His work with Hollywood allowed him to utilize celebrity endorsements and huge advertising campaigns, which spread the allure of noticeable make-up even further. The 1930s had a favoured look which consisted of a natural slightly pink complexion, enhanced by foundations and mauve-coloured powders to create a flawless base. The desire for a waxy look meant many women avoided blushers; however, a very pale pink was the colour of choice if you did opt for a cheek colour. As the decade moved on, there was an influx of orange-tinted foundations and a darker more noticeable blush for the cheeks. From the mid-thirties, lips grew darker in colour and became more defined, which would wonderfully offset the paleness of the face, creating a striking look. The eyebrows were plucked into pencil-thin lines, with some women even opting to shave them off in order to create the perfect brow with a pencil. The brow would extend past its natural start and finish points in order to create a more dramatic visual effect. The eyelids tended to be painted with shades of violet, greens and greys and covered with Vaseline in order to create a wet sheen, similar to the eyebrows and lips. False and curled lashes were also popular in order to widen the eye and enhance the dramatic look that had been created.

Influence of the 1930s in Later Years

Fashion designers regularly seek inspiration from historical shapes, styles and silhouettes, and can reinterpret and disseminate them to consumers through their catwalk shows. The 1930s had some extremely wearable features that would translate to contemporary taste. The bias cut is still referenced by many designers today, given its classic and figure-accentuating effect. The incorporation of these historical influences is often a mode in which to make a deeper commentary about their contemporary era by referencing the ideals and influences of the past, as noted by Lorynn Divita in 2010.

Divita explores theoretical concepts such as 'Nystrom's Zeitgeist' and 'Laver's Law', which focus on demonstrating society's 'gaps in appreciation' when concerning historic fashion styles. Laver explores the notion that society has a habit of viewing contemporary fashions as exemplary. In Laver's timeline, innovative looks are first considered daring and it is only as they approach acceptance by a mass audience that they are considered appropriate. As a fashion passes it is considered dowdy when it is in the very recent past, then eventually it becomes admired again. This law is intended to be utilized by observers of fashion to unpick the commentary a designer is making by incorporating retro fashions in his or her creations, perhaps encouraging a greater appreciation of historically inspired fashion. At the time of writing the thirties are experiencing a reinvigoration of appreciation and study within both fashion and fashion history. This could be due to the elegance associated within such clothing, but also to the references designers are making to the socio-political context of the thirties, a troubled decade in crisis that saw design and creativity flourish.

The incorporation of historical influences into contemporary collections often has more than purely aesthetic meanings. Designers may well be attempting to convey an additional message through the stylistic features or eras they reference in their work. This theory is defined by Ingrid Brenninkmeyer as 'historic continuity', which she claims as the steady evolution of clothing, with reference to the continual recurrence of styles, symbolism and decorative elements that are frequently employed by designers in their collections. If this is the case, then contemporary designers may be commenting on current political or social events by drawing inspiration from or referencing stylistic features from other eras that suffered similar socio-political turbulence or prosperity.

This is unpicked further if contemporary fashion that contains historical references is viewed through the concept of the 'zeitgeist' or spirit of the times as Nystrom defines it, based on a selection of factors that might guide the character of this zeitgeist. This allows the viewer to consider the deeper significance of the commentary made by the designer.

Conclusion

The 1930s was a time of contradictions and crisis. It is remembered for the economic crisis and Great Depression experienced after the Wall Street Crash in 1929, for the declaring of WWII, and for the innovative and liberating changes in fashion design, art and architecture. If one is to assume that with economic downturns the development of fashion, design and art would halt, then the decade turns this notion on its head. This era was one of fruitful change and liberation for the female form. The environment for creativity in Paris at this time was vibrant and rich, with a huge variety of creative methods, from designing to styling; the parallel development of art movements and the artists that followed them illustrates what was so unique about the 1930s. Prominent designers such as Coco Chanel and Madeleine Vionnet have a special place in fashion history for their innovative yet differing ways of working: they are remembered as trailblazers for very different reasons, but they both created new and exciting ways for lovers of fashion to express themselves.

The ready-to-wear revolution democratized fashion, allowing more people from across the class spectrum to enjoy, embrace and dabble in new trends and styles of clothing. Technological advancements in fabric production and creation ensured this market could flourish and created a stronger fashion industry for all. The ease with which the wealthy could now vacation and travel saw the development of resort wear, with boundaries being pushed further than ever before on the decks of the cruise ships that were populating the ocean. Activewear was hugely popularized and improved, providing functional and fashionable attire for those now taking part in sports and sporting events. The newly liberated and refined body required physical exercise, which saw an increase in participation in sporting activity and physical fitness.

Although an era of crisis, the 1930s was an age of elegance redefining the female form, freeing it from its restrictive undergarments. Never before did a decade in fashion history make such radical changes in design, style and social propriety, with the body being slowly liberated from the shackles of previous fashions. Although there are other decades that could lay claim to making such innovative and lasting changes within the environment of fashion, the 1930s has an inherent timelessness that still enchants today.

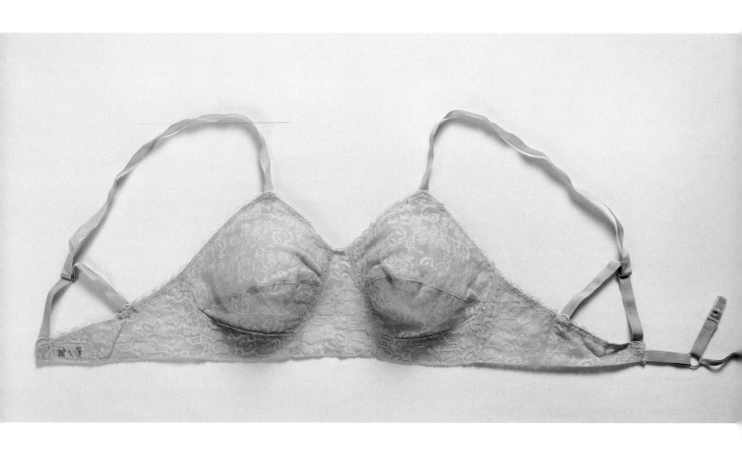

Lingerie Set

4

This beautifully delicate set of lingerie is part of a trousseau collection and comprises a soft, non-wired cotton lace brassiere, a pair of silk satin, lace-trimmed high-leg knickers and a pair of silk, lace-trimmed French-style knickers.

The brassiere is made by a company called Venus and is soft-structured in pink stretch lace, lined with pink tulle net and trimmed with ivory scalloped-edge narrow lace. The shoulder straps are of pink grosgrain ribbon attached to an elastic adjuster loop which is stitched to the back of the bust band. The brassiere fastens at the back with a hook that attaches through a bound eyelet on a pink velvet ribbon strap.

The high-leg knickers are of ivory silk satin and have an unlined gusset. The nude-coloured, corded stretch lace inserts at the sides of the knickers are pleated at the waist to allow for movement. They fasten at the left side with a hook and bar placket. The knickers are virtually seamless with attractively hemstitched edges.

The French-style knickers are of ivory silk, with nude-coloured, corded stretch lace which has been hand-stitched to the leg openings, with cut-away detailing. The knickers are structured with a pointed waist panel, gusset panel and straight, shorts-style legs. They are fastened at the waist with a single mother-of-pearl button on each side.

These intricately stitched pieces would work well in any colour combination, but the knickers work best with light, silk fabrics as these will provide the softness and fluidity essential to this type of garment.

MEASUREMENTS

Brassiere: Bust 81 cm (32in), approximate cup size A

High-leg knickers: Waist 61 cm (24in), Hips 81.5cm (32in)

French-style knickers: Waist 61 cm (24in), Hips 81.5cm (32in)

Approximate size: UK 8, US 4, EU 36

Instructions for Making Up the Lingerie Set

To start

Begin by cutting out all the pattern pieces for the lingerie set, adding seam allowances, and set them aside.

Making Up the Brassiere

Making up the bust cups and under-bust bands

(1) To start, make up the lace bust cups and their tulle linings. With right sides together, stitch along the centre cup seams (marked A on the pattern). Trim the allowance to approximately 0.7cm (¼in) and press the seams to face down toward the lower edges of the bust

Bust cup seam, from the right side.

FABRIC SUGGESTIONS AND NOTIONS

Soft, lightweight fabrics that feel comfortable against the skin are best for making lingerie. The brassiere will require a stretch fabric to achieve the closest fit. Stretch lace lined with lingerie net would work perfectly; for a touch of pure luxury, an alternative option would be to use a stretch silk charmeuse. The knickers would work well with any lightweight silk or satin fabrics and a nice touch for the high-leg knickers side inserts would be to use the same stretch lace as the brassiere.

Brassiere:

2 x 1.5cm (⅝in) rectangular bra adjusters

1 x 1.5cm (⅝in) diameter circular bra adjuster

1 x 1cm (⅜in) hook

73cm (29in) of 1cm (⅜in) wide grosgrain ribbon

6.5cm (2½ in) of 1cm (⅜in) wide velvet ribbon

73.5cm (29in) of 0.7cm (¼in) lace trim

33cm (13in) of 1cm (⅜in) wide elastic

High-leg knickers:

3 x 1cm (⅜in) hooks and bars

French-style knickers:

2 x 1.2cm (½in) diameter mother-of-pearl buttons

Left: Pink Venus stretch lace brassiere. French-style knickers.

cups. Next, and with right sides together, place each lace cup onto its corresponding tulle lining, ensuring that the central cup seams are aligned. Stitch along the top edges of each cup, trim the allowance to approximately 0.7cm (¼in) and turn out. Press the finished top edge to create a clean, crisp line.

The bust seams can now be reinforced by machine top-stitching through all the layers, making sure the lace and tulle seams are aligned and the layers of fabric are lying smoothly.
(2) Next, the inner cup linings must be attached. Begin by laying the sections onto the inside of the bust cups, line up the centre edges (marked C on the pattern) and tack or machine stay-stitch into position.
(3) Turn under 0.7cm (¼in) of fabric along the long, curved edge of the lining sections and stitch onto the bust cups through all the layers. Press to finish.
(4) The under-bust bands can now be attached to the bust cups. Start by taking each section and press lightly along the centre, to create the lower edge fold. Next, on the inside of each cup and with the right sides together, attach one curved edge of the band to the lower edge of the cup (marked B on the pattern). Stitch together and trim the seam allowance to approximately 0.7cm (¼in). Fold back and press the seam down, away from the bust cup.
(5) Next, bring the remaining free edge of the band to the front, turn under sufficient seam allowance so that the folded edge of the band lies 0.7cm (¼in) above the raw edge of the bust cup and is aligned with the inside seam. Machine top-stitch through all the layers to secure. Press to finish.

Making up and attaching the centre front panel

(6) To create the centre front panel, begin by taking the lace and tulle sections and, with right sides together, stitch along the upper and lower edges to create two seams. Trim the allowances to approximately 0.7cm (¼in) and turn out. Press both edges to finish.
(7) Now the bust cups can be attached to the panel. With right sides together, position each cup either side of the centre front band (marked C on the pattern), stitch into place through all the layers, then press the seam allowances in toward the cups. Finally, machine two parallel rows of top-stitching along both seams, approximately 0.3cm (⅛in) apart and securing all the layers.

On the inside of the panel, trim back the excess fabric on the seam allowances close to the stitching lines and press to finish.

Making up and attaching the side bands

(8) Follow the same instructions as for making up the centre front panel and attach each side band to the outer edges of the bust cup section (marked D on the pattern).

Bust cup lining, from the inside.

Bust cup lining, from the right side.

Attaching the lace trim and ribbon straps

(9) Working on the inside of the brassiere, position the lace trim along the entire top edge with approximately 0.3cm (⅛in) of the lace showing above the seam line.

(10) If a slightly wider lace trim has been chosen, then go by the design and depth of pattern to ascertain how much lace should show. Once the trim is positioned evenly along the edge, attach using two rows of parallel machine top-stitching, approximately 0.3cm (⅛in) apart.

(11) To create the shoulder straps, begin by cutting two 36.5cm (14½in) lengths of the grosgrain ribbon. On one end of each piece, attach a rectangular lingerie adjuster by threading the ribbon through the loop, leaving approximately 1.8cm (¾in) to attach to the brassiere, and tuck under 0.7cm (¼in). Machine top-stitch around the end of the ribbon in a rectangular shape to secure.

(12) Once complete, lay each section of ribbon flat, with the turned edge facing down, and attach the unfinished end of the ribbon to the inside of the upper edge of the bust cup where it comes to a point. Turn under 0.7cm (¼in) and either hand-sew or machine-stitch into place. If stitching by machine, take care to follow the stitching lines used to attach the lace trim as this will give a neat and professional finish.

Under-bust band, from the inside.

Under-bust band, from the right side.

Centre front panel, from the right side.

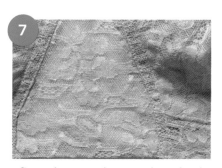

Centre front panel, top-stitching detail.

Side band, from the right side.

Lace trim attached on the inside.

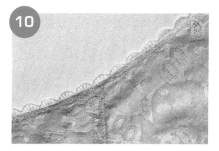

Lace trim, from the right side.

Shoulder strap adjuster detail.

Shoulder strap attachment to bust cup on the inside.

Attaching the elastic and fastenings

(13) The next step is to attach the elastic adjustment loops and back strap fastening. Start by creating the elastic loops that attach to the upper edges of the side panels. Cut two pieces of elastic approximately 18cm (7in) long and, starting at the ends of each side strap, position one end of the elastic on the inside of the brassiere 1cm (⅜in) down from the edge at the point marked on the pattern and stitch neatly into place either by hand or machine. Thread the free end of the elastic through the lingerie adjuster on the ribbon strap and attach in the same manner as before at the second point marked on the pattern. Make sure that the ribbon strap is not twisted as the elastic is pulled through the adjuster.

(14) To create the back fastening, take the circular lingerie adjuster and thread through two 10cm (4in) pieces of elastic and double them over to form two horizontal straps, approximately 4cm (1½in) plus turnings. Next, turn under the seam allowance at the end of the left-hand side panel of the brassiere and stitch one of the elastic loops to this, securing through all the layers. Finish on the inside of the brassiere by hand-stitching a small section of tulle to cover the raw ends of the elastic. Press lightly to finish.

(15) The right-hand side of the back fastening can now be completed. Start by preparing the small velvet ribbon strap that will attach to the elastic loop. Cut a piece of ribbon approximately 6.5cm (2½in) long and, using a hole punch or tailor's awl, make a small hole at one end, 0.3cm (⅛in) in diameter and approximately 1.5cm (⅝in) in from the raw edge. Finish the hole by hand, using a close, neat buttonhole stitch. Fold the ribbon in half and, with the hole uppermost, attach it to the free end of the second elastic loop, stitching securely by hand or machine through all the layers.

(16) Note: the narrow, pink elastic loop which hangs vertically from the bra adjuster ring is an optional addition. Originally it would probably have been used to attach the brassiere to a corset. To create the strap, simply take a 7.5cm (3in) section of 0.7cm (¼in) elastic, loop through the adjuster ring and stitch a 1cm (⅜in) metal hook at the end.

(17) Finally, finish the right-hand side fastening by either applying one hook from a section of corset fastening tape, inside the end of the right-hand side panel, or, if preferred, simply turn under the raw edge, attach a 1cm (⅜in) hook and cover with a small section of tulle to neaten, matching the finish of the left-hand side of the fastening.

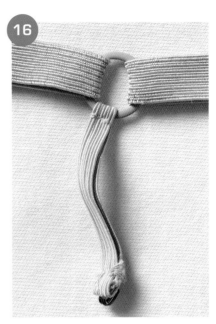

Corset strap detail.

Elastic loop adjuster detail on the side band.

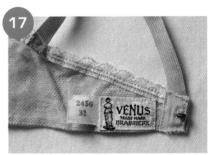

Right-hand side fastening, from the inside.

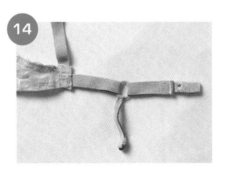

Back fastening detail.

Velvet strap showing buttonhole.

Making Up the High-Leg Knickers

Attaching the lace edging

(18) To begin with, the narrow lace trim must be attached along each edge that will go on to form the knickers leg openings. On the original garment, the lace has been applied by machine using an heirloom stitch, or Venetian hem.

As an alternative to using an heirloom stitch, a neat finish can be achieved by simply turning under approximately 0.7cm (¼in) to the wrong side along each leg opening.

Press to create a sharp edge and then lay this edge onto the right side of the lace trim and attach by using a straight or zig-zag machine-stitch. Ensure that the chosen stitch is small and neat in order to achieve the delicate appearance of fine lingerie. Hand-stitching the lace into place would work just as well.

Once the lace is applied, trim down any excess fabric on the inside of the knickers to neaten and press lightly to finish.

Attaching the lace side inserts

(19) Start by attaching a lace section onto the side seams of the knickers in the same manner as the lace trim on the leg openings.

(20) At this point, the knickers will be completely joined with no opening at the waistband and the lace inserts left unpleated. Next, create the left side opening by first cutting a 9cm (3½in) vertical slit down the lace, approximately 1.2cm (½in) in from the seam where the lace and the front knickers panel are joined.

(21) At the base of the newly cut opening, fold a small pleat approximately 1.2cm (½in) on the double and secure across the pleat using a few small, straight stitches through all the layers.

(22) Now the placket opening can be created. On the fabric edge, simply turn under the lace to the seam line and, on the wrong side, turn under a small hem and hand-sew the lace to the silk satin using a slip-stitch.

(23) The lace side of the placket opening is finished simply by turning under a hem, approximately 0.3cm (⅛in) on the double, which is secured by slip-stitching by hand.

(24) Next, fold the box pleats to the marks indicated on the pattern and machine stay-stitch or tack them in place to hold. The top edge of the lace insert should now measure

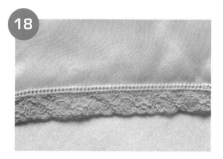

Heirloom stitch, detail.

Heirloom stitch at lace insert.

Side opening, detail.

Side opening, pleat detail inside.

Right side opening at waist, detail of finishing on the inside.

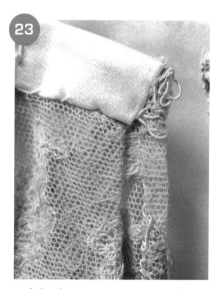

Left side opening at waist, detail of finishing on the inside.

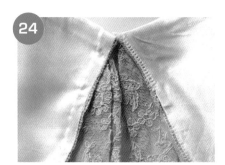

Top edge detail of lace insert.

Waist binding detail, from the right side and inside.

Bar spacing on the side opening.

Side opening detail, from the right side.

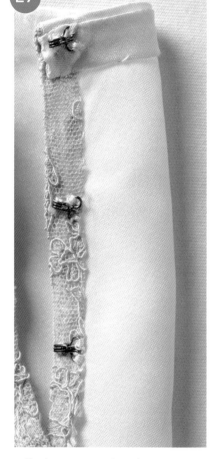

Hook spacing on the side opening.

Completed side opening.

approximately 2.5–3.5cm (1–1⅜in).
(25) Create the box pleats on the right-hand side lace insert by folding the pleats to the marks indicated on the pattern. As before, machine stay-stitch or tack to hold. On this side, the edges of the knickers fabric should meet.

Attaching the waist facing and finishing

(26) Once both lace inserts are complete, the waist can be finished by applying a facing using satin bias binding or a self-binding using a bias-cut strip of the knickers fabric. With right sides together, lay the binding along the top outer edge of the waist, aligning the raw edges, and then stitch into position approximately 0.3cm (⅛in) down from the edge. Fold the attached binding to the inside of the knickers, lining up the seam line along the top edge of the waist, and press. Attach the lower edge of the binding to the knickers by hand using a slip-stitch. If a self-binding is used, a small hem will need to be folded under before sewing. Press to finish.

(27) Finally, finish the closure at the left side of the waist by sewing three hooks on the front side of the opening with one placed at the top edge and the other two spaced evenly down the opening.

(28) On the lace side, stitch the corresponding bars as follows: the top edge bar should be at the waist, positioned approximately 0.3cm (⅛in) in from the seam where the lace and fabric meet; the second bar should be approximately 1cm (⅜in) in from the edge of the placket and the third bar approximately 0.7cm (¼in) in from the edge of the placket.

(29) Once fastened, the left side opening should match the right, with the top point edges of the knickers fabric meeting.

Making Up the French-Style Knickers

Making up the knickers legs

(30) Begin by creating the darts on the two back leg panels. Stitch the darts as indicated on the pattern and press them out toward the side seams. Join the front and back leg panels together at the side seams to the marks indicated on the pattern and at the inside leg seams. The method used is a French seam, as instructed below.

(31) Start creating this twice-stitched seam by placing the wrong sides of the fabric together and stitching the seam in the usual manner, after which the seam is pressed open. Next, trim both raw edges of the seam allowance to approximately 1cm (⅜in): this will ensure that no fibres protrude from the finished French seam on the right side of the fabric.

The second stage in creating the seam is to fold the fabric back on itself, so the right sides are now facing one another and the raw edges of the first seam are completely enclosed. Stitch a

Back panel dart, detail from the right side.

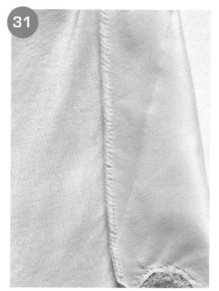

French seam, detail on the inside.

0.7cm (¼in) wide seam and finish by pressing the seam toward the back of the garment.

Inserting the gusset section

(32) Start by taking both gusset sections; on the wrong side, turn under 0.7cm (¼in) seam allowance around the entire outer edges of the pattern pieces (this will, in effect, create a single layer hem). Press to create a sharp fold and try to be as neat and accurate as possible at this stage, as the two sections that make up the finished gusset will be attached simultaneously and stitched through. Where the gusset sections narrow to almost a point, it may be necessary to trim and clip when turning the seam allowance under in order to reduce bulk.

Once both sections have been prepared, take the knickers and, working on the right side to begin with, take one of the gusset sections and lay it onto the knickers at the marks indicated on the pattern. Place the folded edge of the gusset section 0.7cm (¼in) in from the raw edge of the knickers fabric and pin or tack the piece into position.

(33) Next, working on the inside of the knickers, take the remaining gusset section (which will form the lining) and position it in the same manner as the right side, taking care to line it up

accurately with the first gusset section.

At this point, tack through all the layers to secure the gusset sections into position for stitching. This process will also indicate where there may be areas that are not completely aligned and can therefore need to be rectified before the pieces are finally stitched. Once satisfied with the positioning of the pieces, the gusset can be machine top-stitched, working from the right side of the knickers and stitching approximately 0.3cm (⅛in) in from the

Gusset detail, from the right side.

Gusset detail, on the inside.

folded edge. This should ensure that all the layers are secured. Any missed areas on the inside of the gusset can always be secured by hand using a slip-stitch. Once stitched, remove the tacking stitches and press to finish.

Joining the front and back waist panels

(34) Begin by taking the front and back waist panels; along the curved lower edges of each piece, turn under a 0.7cm (¼in) seam allowance as previously carried out on the gusset panel. Press to create a crisp fold. Lay the front waist panel onto the front side of the knickers, 0.7cm (¼in) in from the raw edge and lining up the pointed end with the centre of the gusset panel. Overlap it slightly onto the gusset. **(35)** Machine edge-stitch into position and press to finish. Repeat the process for the back waist panel.

Creating the side placket openings

(36) The knickers should now be completely joined with an 11.5cm (4½in) opening at each side. To complete the placket opening, start with the placket facing; fold it in half lengthways, then press. Next, and with right sides together, attach one long edge to the raw edges of the side opening, using a 0.7cm (¼in) seam allowance. Once stitched, press the seam back lightly on the right side and in the direction of the opening. On the remaining long, raw edge, turn under a 0.7cm (¼in) seam allowance and press. The placket should now have one stitched seam, a central fold and a

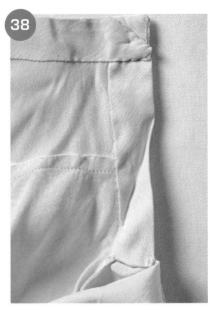

Placket detail from the inside, back waist.

Join of leg with the front waist panel.

Side placket detail at the back waist.

Placket detail from the right side, front waist.

Join of leg with the back waist panel.

Placket detail from the right side, back waist.

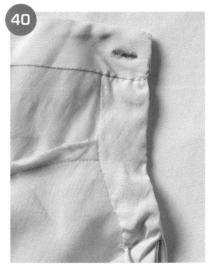

Placket detail from the inside, front waist.

turned, free seam allowance.

(37) Next, complete the back waist panel plackets by attaching the free, turned seam allowance to the stitched seam allowance.

(38,39) Secure by hand using a slip-stitch, but only to the point where the top of the side seam meets the opening.

(40) Finish the front waist panel plackets by turning the entire placket section to the inside of the knickers, so the seamline is lined up with the side seam.

(41) This will create a horizontal fold where the opening meets the top of the side seam. Finish by attaching the free,

Placket base, detail.

Waist facing detail, from the right side and inside.

long edge of the placket to the knickers fabric by hand, using a small, neat slip-stitch. Secure the bottom fold using a few, small straight hand-stitches. Press to finish.

Attaching the waist facings

(42) For the waist facings, begin by cutting two sections of the knickers fabric, on the straight grain and measuring approximately 38cm (15in) long x 5cm (2in) wide. With right sides together and lining up the raw edges, stitch a facing section to the front and back waist panels and trim the seam allowance to approximately 0.3cm (⅛in). Fold to the inside of the knickers so that the seamline lies along the top edge of the waist. Working on the inside of the knickers, fold under the remaining fabric allowance to create a 2.5cm (1in) facing. This should leave a substantial turning inside the facing. Stitch the free edge of the facing to the knickers by hand, using a small, neat slip-stitch.

Tuck the ends of the openings in neatly to finish the facings and plackets, then hand-sew using a slip-stitch. Press to finish. Finally the fastenings can be added to the garment. At the top corner of each of the back waist plackets, attach a button. The buttons on the original garment are of mother of pearl, but a crystal or covered button would work equally well. The important thing to remember is that the chosen button should be flat, in order for the knickers to lie smoothly and comfortably on the body.

(43) At the corresponding points on the front waist plackets, create a horizontal buttonhole, using either a

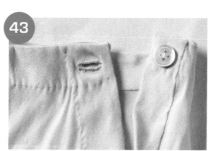

Button and buttonhole fastening.

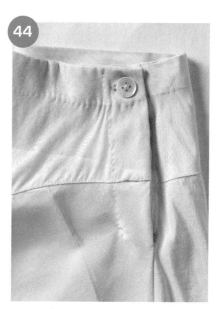

Side opening completed.

machine or hand-stitched method. Make the buttonhole just slightly longer than the diameter of the button, to allow for ease of fit.

(44) The finished plackets should lie smoothly in line with the side seams.

Attaching the lace trim

The final task is to attach the decorative lace trim to finish the knickers leg openings. The original garment uses a deep, stretch lace to enhance the legs and add to the luxurious and romantic feel of the piece. This has been achieved by using a stitch and cut-away method of application, which softens the hard edge of the hemline.

Begin by studying the pattern of the chosen lace and noting where it repeats, rises and falls.

(45) Working on the right side of the fabric and using the lowest points of the scalloped or shaped edge of the lace as a guide, lay the lace, right side uppermost, along the knickers fabric at the leg opening. Make sure that the lowest points are positioned 0.7cm (¼in) above the raw edge of the knickers leg hemlines. Trim around the pattern, leaving 0.7cm (¼in) allowance to tuck under.

Lay the lace all the way around the leg openings, starting and ending at the inside leg seams. Take time to ensure the lace lies flat and evenly onto the knickers fabric and secure into position using a tacking stitch. Stitch around the lace, following the shape of the pattern, leaving enough space to turn the lace under when finishing.

(46) Join the inside leg seams of the lace by laying the front allowance over the back, to ensure it sits flat and without bulk. Hand-stitch together and trim away any excess.

(47) Next, turn under the seam allowance on the lace edge and attach to the knickers either by hand, using a small, neat overcast stitch, or by machine if it has an embroidery foot and available stitches. Take care when stitching to keep the fabric and lace at an even tension.

(48) Finally, trim away excess fabric on the inside of the knickers legs to leave an allowance of approximately 0.3cm (⅛in) to complete the cut-away effect. Press carefully to finish.

Lace hem detail on the leg opening.

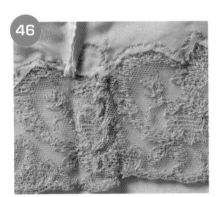

Inside leg seam, detail.

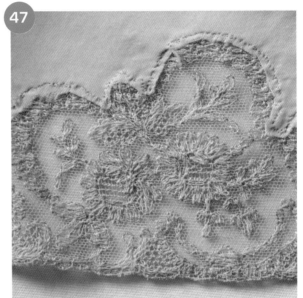

Lace hem, from the inside.

Lace hem, finished effect, from the right side.

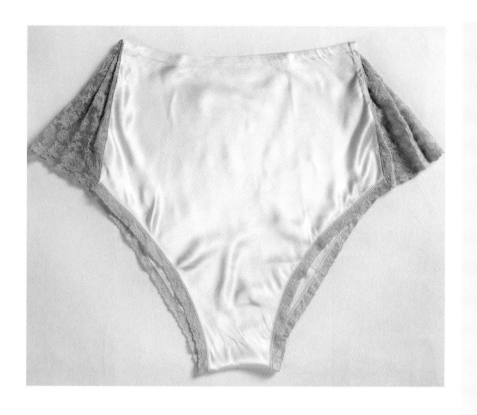

When opting for vintage-inspired underwear, you might want to consider incorporating these garments into an evening or party look, wearing items of underwear as outerwear. Given the changes in style and coverage, some soft thirties-inspired bra tops might make for a fun and feminine contemporary crop top worn with a pair of jeans, or worn over a black roll neck if you are looking for more coverage. This use of underwear as outerwear allows you to incorporate interesting fabrics such as laces and silks into your look. The simplicity and delicate nature of thirties-inspired underwear will ensure it is timeless and could be incorporated into your look for years to come.

High-leg silk satin knickers, detail.

BRASSIERE
SCALE 1:1 FOR ALL PATTERN PIECES ON THIS PAGE

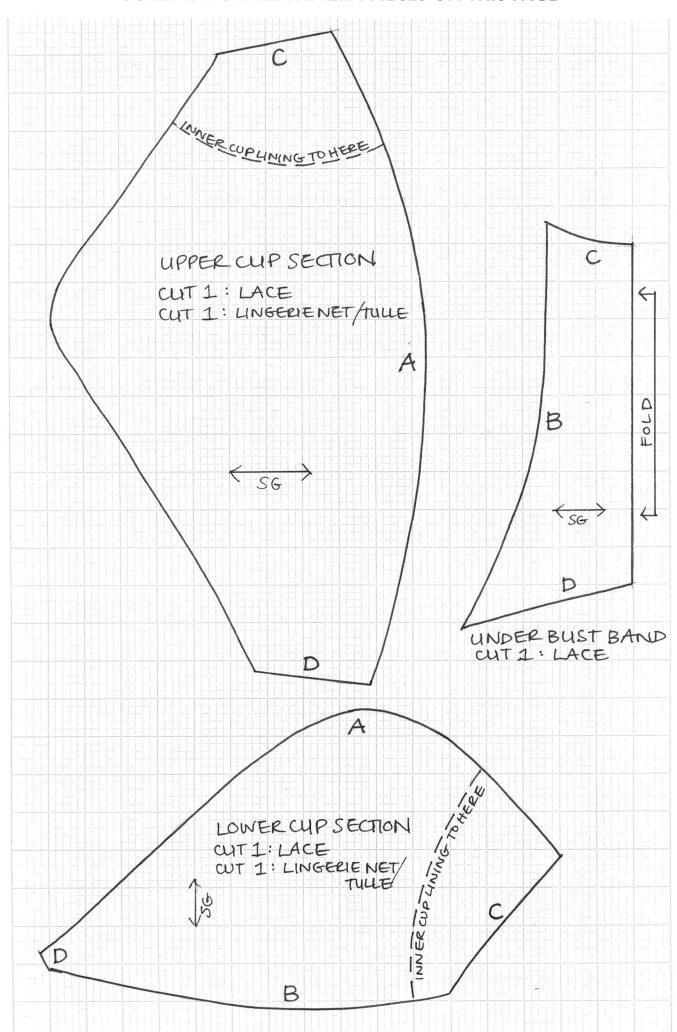

C

INNER CUP LINING TO HERE

UPPER CUP SECTION

CUT 1 : LACE
CUT 1 : LINGERIE NET/TULLE

A

SG

D

C

B

SG

FOLD

D

UNDER BUST BAND
CUT 1 : LACE

A

LOWER CUP SECTION
CUT 1: LACE
CUT 1: LINGERIE NET/TULLE

SG

INNER CUP LINING TO HERE

C

D

B

BRASSIERE
SCALE 1:1 FOR ALL PATTERN PIECES ON THIS PAGE

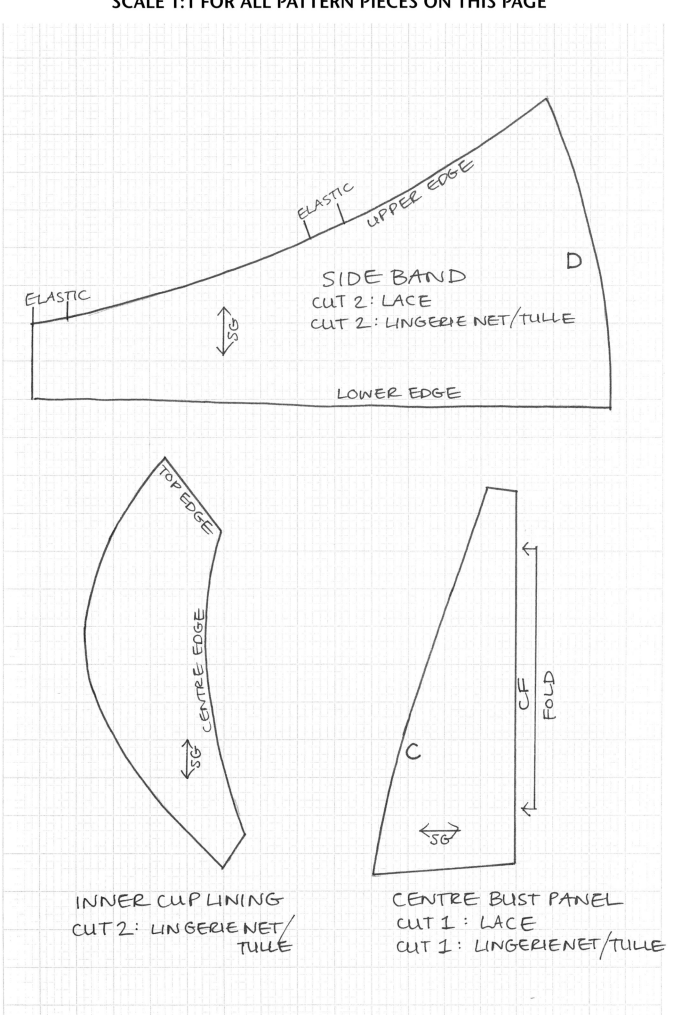

ELASTIC

UPPER EDGE

SIDE BAND
CUT 2: LACE
CUT 2: LINGERIE NET/TULLE

D

ELASTIC

SG

LOWER EDGE

TOP EDGE

CENTRE EDGE

SG

INNER CUP LINING
CUT 2: LINGERIE NET/
TULLE

CF FOLD

C

SG

CENTRE BUST PANEL
CUT 1: LACE
CUT 1: LINGERIE NET/TULLE

HIGH LEG KNICKERS
SCALE 1:5 FOR ALL PATTERN PIECES ON THIS PAGE

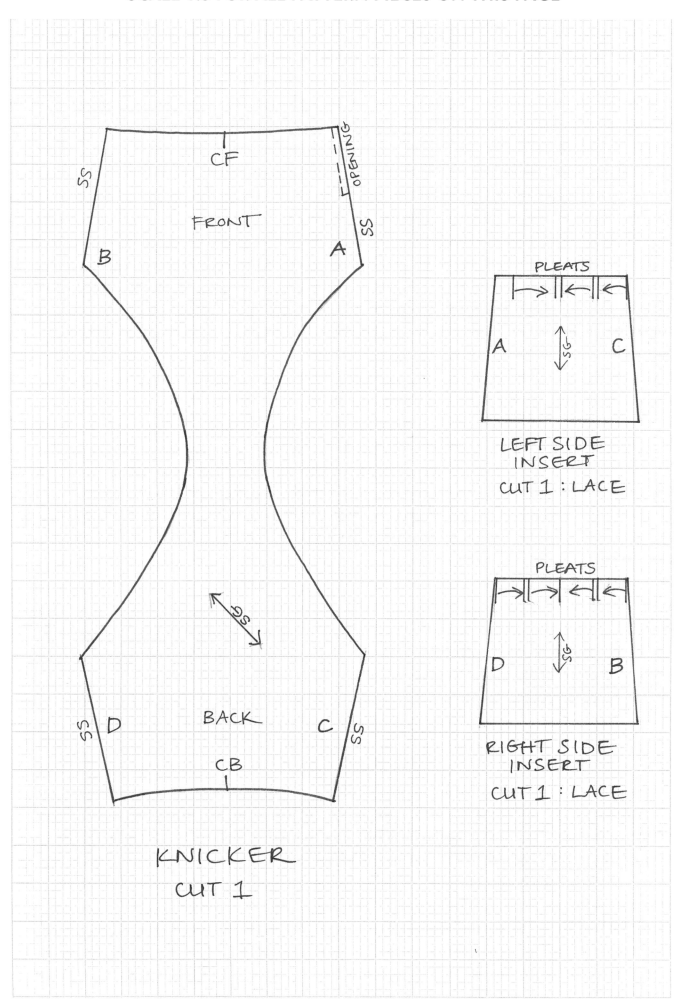

SS

CF

OPENING

SS

FRONT

B

A

SS

SS

D

BACK

C

SS

CB

KNICKER

CUT 1

PLEATS

A

SG

C

LEFT SIDE
INSERT
CUT 1 : LACE

PLEATS

D

SG

B

RIGHT SIDE
INSERT
CUT 1 : LACE

FRENCH STYLE KNICKERS
SCALE 1:5 FOR ALL PATTERN PIECES ON THIS PAGE

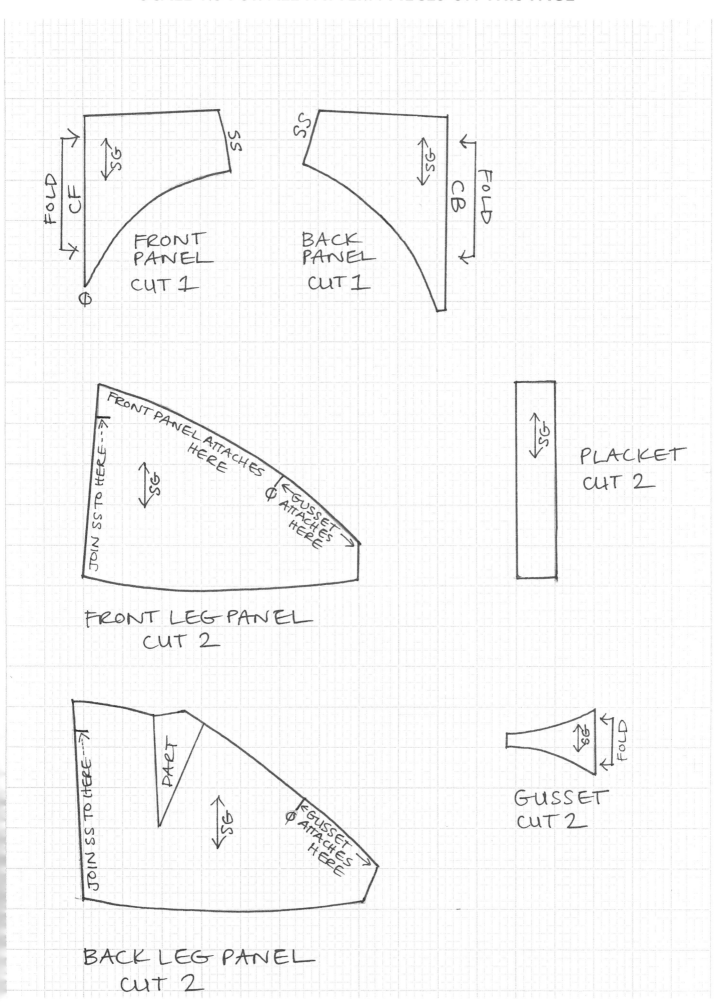

Kimono Robe

5

This light and elegant piece has simple lines and is cut from one folded section of lightweight, printed silk with a stylized floral motif. The three-quarter-length sleeves are attached separately. An applied, wide band of the silk fabric around the front opening and neckline provides the finishing and there are no fastenings. The sleeve cuffs are simply faced, using a fine, wide cotton tape. Although the kimono robe has been stitched by machine, the very fine silk thread that has been used renders the stitches almost invisible. The various repairs to the stitching indicate that this was a well-loved garment and also acts as a reminder of the delicate nature of the fabric.

Any fine silk type, such as pongee, or a lightweight cotton fabric would be suitable to make the robe, but if a fabric that allows for the incorporation of a hemline border is chosen (as can be seen on the original garment), then the shoulders will need to be seamed to allow for the correct placement of any design. The folded, all-in-one pattern would be suitable for a fabric with general, all-over design with no obvious or defined direction of decoration.

Back of silk kimono robe.

Left: Silk kimono robe.

To start

Begin by cutting out all the pattern pieces for the kimono robe, adding seam allowances, and set them aside.

Joining the side seams

(1) The kimono robe is created using enclosed seams which are stitched in the following manner. With right sides together, join the side seams by first hand-sewing a line of running stitches along each seam, 0.7cm (¼in) in from the raw edges and to the marks indicated on the pattern.

Next, trim the allowance to approximately 0.3cm (⅛in), then fold the edges over so that the stitching line is positioned along the seam edge and press flat. To complete the seam and enclose the raw edges, fold the

Seam detail from the inside.

MEASUREMENTS

Across the chest: 122cm (48in)

The loose styling of this garment means that the kimono robe described here would comfortably fit the following sizes: UK 10/12, US 6/8, EU 38/40

FABRIC SUGGESTIONS AND NOTIONS

The robe would have traditionally been made using pongee silk, a popular fabric of the era, but any fine lightweight silk would be suitable. Alternatively, a lightweight satin would work nicely, as would a lightweight cotton fabric, such as cotton lawn.

Fine silk or polyester thread

107cm (42in) of 10cm (4in) wide fine cotton or linen tape

allowance over again to create a finished width of 0.7cm (¼in) and machine-stitch through all the layers, along the edge of the inner fold. Finish by pressing the seam toward the back of the robe.

If preferred, as an alternative to the enclosed seam technique, the robe can be created using French seams, following the method outlined in the previous chapter.
Note: If a shoulder seam is required, join using the same method.

Making up the sleeves and attaching the facings

(2) Take each sleeve pattern piece and join the seams in the same manner as for the side seams. Once the sleeve seams have been stitched and pressed, the facings can be attached to the hem

Sleeve facing, seam detail on the inside.

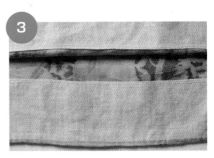

Sleeve facing, top-stitching detail on the inside.

Sleeve facing, top-stitching detail from the right side.

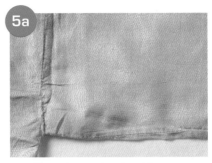

Sleeve inserted at the side seam.

Sleeve inserted, from the inside.

openings. Take a section of the facing tape, approximately 53.5cm (21in) long (including 2.5cm (1in) for seam allowance). With right sides together, place the facing onto the hem opening, lining up the raw edges and ensuring the join in the tape will align with the sleeve seam join.

Starting and finishing 2.5cm (1in) either side of the sleeve seam, stitch the facing onto the hem opening, 0.7cm (¼in) in from the raw edges. Once attached, the free ends of the facing can be joined to create a seam, then stitch the remainder of the facing to the hem opening. Press the facing join flat.
(3) The next stage is to fold the facing back into the sleeve, leaving approximately 0.3cm (⅛in) of the sleeve fabric showing above the facing tape seam. Press the edge to create a defined edge. To finish the facing, top-stitch the free edge of the facing tape onto the sleeve.
(4) Using a fine thread will ensure the stitches are not too obvious on the right side of the sleeve.

For a couture finish, the facing could be attached using a slip-stitch from the wrong side or a prick-stitch from the right side. Press lightly to finish.

Inserting the sleeves into the kimono robe
(5) The kimono sleeves are simply inserted by placing the right sides of the fabric together and aligning the sleeve seam to the side seam and the upper fold of the sleeve with the shoulder line, indicated on the pattern. Stitch the sleeve onto the kimono robe using the method previously used to create the side and sleeve seams.
(6) Press to finish.

Kimono sleeve attached, from the right side.

Finishing the hem
(7) The narrow hem of the kimono must be finished before the front facing band can be added. Start by making a double turning of 0.7cm (¼in) to create a narrow, enclosed hem. Top-stitch all the way along the hem, just below the turned edge. Press to finish

Kimono hem detail.

Attaching the neck/opening binding
The all-in-one neck and front opening binding is created by first cutting a long narrow section of the kimono fabric using the pattern. This section of fabric, which is cut on the straight grain, should measure 107.5cm (42in) long x 10cm (4in) wide. As an alternative to using the kimono robe

fabric, a contrasting or complementary plain, lightweight silk could be used to striking effect.
(8) Once the section has been cut, begin by folding it in half lengthways and with right side outermost. Press along the length to create a crisp fold. Next, and with right sides together, place one raw edge of the binding around the kimono's front opening and neckline. It is a good idea to start at the centre back neck and work from this point down each side of the kimono opening. This will ensure the binding is attached evenly without pulling or puckering.

Stitch into place 0.7cm (¼in) in from the raw edges and then press the binding back toward the centre front.
(9) Finally, working on the inside, finish

Centre back neck, detail.

Hem binding detail, from the inside.

the binding by folding under a 0.7cm (¼in) turning, lining up the folded edge with the seam stitches, and tuck the remaining allowance in at the hem edge.

Working on the right side, machine top-stitch to secure all the layers and press to finish. If preferred, the inside turning can be attached by hand, using a slip-stitch. Press lightly to finish.

Fabric detail of silk kimono robe.

STYLE GUIDE

The simplicity and versatility of the kimono renders this garment a wonderful addition to any outfit or wardrobe. The loose-fitting nature of the garment allows you to wear it over many other outfits, and even provides you with the option of using a belt to cinch it into the waist, wearing it like a shirt or a belted top. The combination of patterns and colours in which you could make this garment gives you the choice as to where and how you would wear it. You might opt for an interesting metallic or iridescent fabric if you are looking for an evening look, reserving simple patterns, florals and silks for daytime chic.

Shoulder detail of silk kimono robe.

Kimono Robe

This light and elegant piece has simple lines and is cut from one folded section of lightweight, printed silk with a stylized floral motif. The three-quarter-length sleeves are attached separately. An applied, wide band of the silk fabric around the front opening and neckline provides the finishing and there are no fastenings. The sleeve cuffs are simply faced, using a fine, wide cotton tape. Although the kimono robe has been stitched by machine, the very fine silk thread that has been used renders the stitches almost invisible. The various repairs to the stitching indicate that this was a well-loved garment and also acts as a reminder of the delicate nature of the fabric.

Any fine silk type, such as pongee, or a lightweight cotton fabric would be suitable to make the robe, but if a fabric that allows for the incorporation of a hemline border is chosen (as can be seen on the original garment), then the shoulders will need to be seamed to allow for the correct placement of any design. The folded, all-in-one pattern would be suitable for a fabric with general, all-over design with no obvious or defined direction of decoration.

Back of silk kimono robe.

Left: Silk kimono robe.

Instructions for Making Up the Kimono Robe

To start
Begin by cutting out all the pattern pieces for the kimono robe, adding seam allowances, and set them aside.

Joining the side seams
(1) The kimono robe is created using enclosed seams which are stitched in the following manner. With right sides together, join the side seams by first hand-sewing a line of running stitches along each seam, 0.7cm (¼in) in from the raw edges and to the marks indicated on the pattern.

Next, trim the allowance to approximately 0.3cm (⅛in), then fold the edges over so that the stitching line is positioned along the seam edge and press flat. To complete the seam and enclose the raw edges, fold the

Seam detail from the inside.

6 STEPS TO CREATE A 1930s KIMONO ROBE

1. Cut out all the pattern pieces

2. Join the side seams

3. Make up the sleeves and attach the facings

4. Insert the sleeves into the kimono robe

5. Finish the hem

6. Attach the front opening/neckline binding

MEASUREMENTS

Across the chest: 122cm (48in)

The loose styling of this garment means that the kimono robe described here would comfortably fit the following sizes: UK 10/12, US 6/8, EU 38/40

FABRIC SUGGESTIONS AND NOTIONS

The robe would have traditionally been made using pongee silk, a popular fabric of the era, but any fine lightweight silk would be suitable. Alternatively, a lightweight satin would work nicely, as would a lightweight cotton fabric, such as cotton lawn.

Fine silk or polyester thread

107cm (42in) of 10cm (4in) wide fine cotton or linen tape

allowance over again to create a finished width of 0.7cm (¼in) and machine-stitch through all the layers, along the edge of the inner fold. Finish by pressing the seam toward the back of the robe.

If preferred, as an alternative to the enclosed seam technique, the robe can be created using French seams, following the method outlined in the previous chapter.
Note: If a shoulder seam is required, join using the same method.

Making up the sleeves and attaching the facings
(2) Take each sleeve pattern piece and join the seams in the same manner as for the side seams. Once the sleeve seams have been stitched and pressed, the facings can be attached to the hem

Sleeve facing, seam detail on the inside.

Sleeve facing, top-stitching detail on the inside.

Sleeve facing, top-stitching detail from the right side.

Sleeve inserted at the side seam.

Sleeve inserted, from the inside.

KIMONO ROBE
1:10 FOR ALL PATTERN PIECES ON THIS PAGE

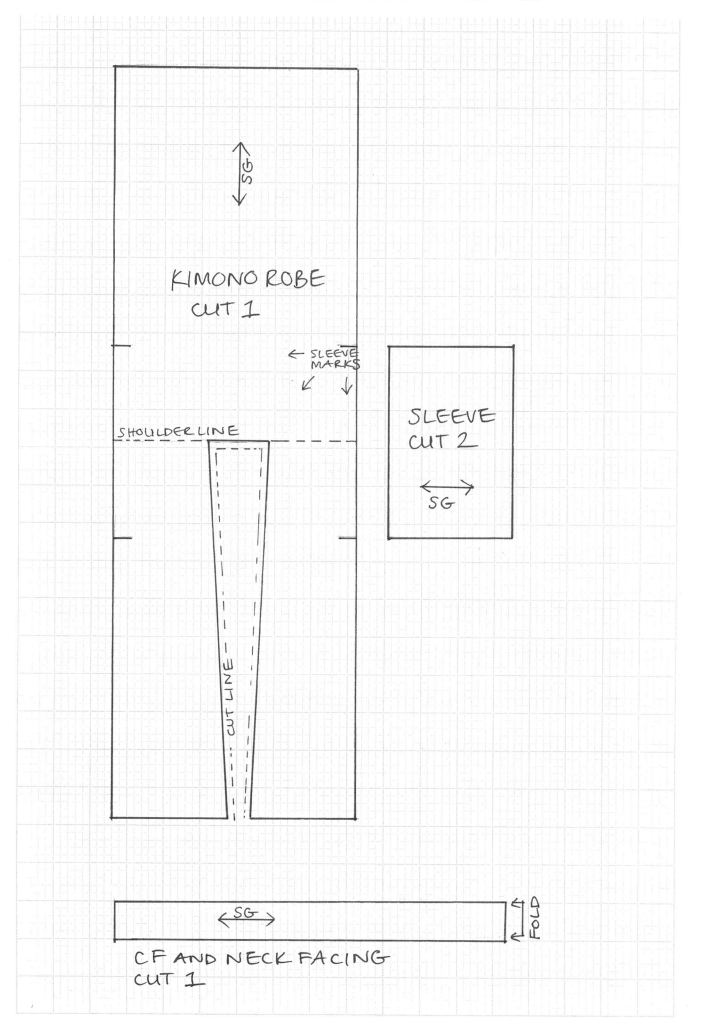

Playsuit

6

This sophisticated yet flirtatious all-in-one playsuit forms part of a bridal trousseau collection and is of pale green satin crêpe fabric, which is lightweight but with sufficient body to create the soft yet structured look of the piece. The top consists of a high-necked sleeveless bodice with low back and wide shoulder straps. A large bow softens the neckline and adds a decorative element of flamboyance to the otherwise simple styling. The edges are bound using the satin crêpe fabric. All internal seams are finished by hand using an overcast stitch.

The wide-legged trousers attach at the waist and the suit fastens at the centre back with a hook and bar placket. The playsuit is finished with a wide sash which ties at the waist, through self-fabric loops. The choice of a soft, satin fabric imparts a subtle sheen that adds a hint of glamour.

Back of green silk playsuit.

Left: Green silk playsuit.

Instructions for Making Up the Playsuit

To start

Begin by cutting out all the pattern pieces for the playsuit, adding seam allowances and 2.5cm (1in) to the bottom of each leg to allow for the hem. Set the pieces aside.

Joining the centre front and centre back trouser seams

(1) Begin constructing the playsuit by

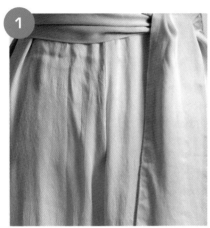

Centre front seam of the trousers, from the right side.

Centre back seam of the trousers, from the right side.

MEASUREMENTS

Bust: 76.5cm (30in)

Waist: 58.5cm (23in)

Hips: 79/81.5cm(31/32in)

Approximate size: UK 6/8, US 2/4, EU 32/36

FABRIC SUGGESTIONS AND NOTIONS

Lightweight silks and satins are ideal for this playsuit. As with the lingerie set, the fabrics will be close to the body and therefore need to be soft and comfortable. Fine, silky jersey knits would also be suitable, but extra care should be taken when stitching due to the extra stretch in the fabric. The playsuit would work well in any colourway.

Matching sewing thread

4 x 1cm (⅜in) hooks and bars

10 STEPS TO CREATE A 1930s PLAYSUIT

1. Cut out all the pattern pieces

2. Join the centre front and centre back trouser seams

3. Join the bodice sections to the trousers

4. Join the inside leg trouser seams and the side seams

5. Finish the trouser leg hems

6. Attach the binding around the bodice

7. Create the centre back placket

8. Make and attach the shoulder straps

9. Make and attach the neck bow

10. Make the waist sash and belt loops

taking the trouser pattern pieces. With right sides together, stitch the two curved seams that will form the centre front and centre back seams of the trouser. Join one seam through its entire length (this will form the centre front) and one seam up to the mark indicated on the pattern at Ø (this will form the centre back). At this stage the curve of the side seams over the hips can be produced by trimming away the excess fabric (shown by hatching on the pattern) leaving a 1.2cm (½in) seam allowance. Stitch the seam and press the edges toward the back of the garment.

(2) There should now be an opening of 11.5 cm (4½in) at the centre back. Trim the seam allowance to 0.7cm (¼in) and neaten by hand using an overcast stitch, ensuring that both raw edges are enclosed.

(3) For the centre back seam, snip diagonally across the seam allowance up toward where the stitching ends and finish the stitched seam allowance in the same manner as the centre front. Press both seams flat, toward one side.

Seam finishing detail of the trousers, on the inside.

Joining the bodice sections to the trousers

(4) Begin by stitching the two front bodice darts and press up toward the neckline when finished.

(5) Take the front bodice section and, with right sides together, join it to the centre front trouser panel, ensuring the centre point of the bodice lines up with the centre front seam.

Stitch the sections together and then trim the seam allowance to 0.7cm (¼in). Finish by hand using an overcast stitch over both raw edges. Press the finished seam down toward the trousers.

(6) Using the same method, attach the two back bodice panels to the back trouser panel and finish as before.

Detail of the finish of the bodice back, on the inside.

Joining the inside leg trouser seams and the side seams

(7) Now that the front and back sections of the playsuit are complete, the next stage is to join the inside leg seam. Lay the panels one on top of the other, with right sides together and ensuring the centre front seams and waist seams are aligned. Stitch around the inside leg seam, making sure the centre front seams meet at the crotch. Stitch both side seams together, matching up the front and back waist seams.

Trim all seam allowances to 0.7cm (¼in) and finish by hand using an overcast stitch over both raw edges. Press the inside leg seam toward the back of the trousers, then press the side seams in the same manner, toward the centre back of the playsuit.

Finishing the trouser leg hems

(8) To finish the trouser leg hems, begin by turning under 0.7cm (¼in) of the allowance and press to create a sharp, crisp edge. Next, turn under another 1.8cm (¾in) to create a hem and sew by hand, using a slip-stitch. Make sure the stitches are neat and barely visible on the right side.

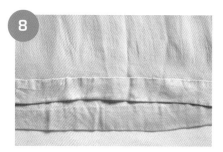

Trouser hem detail, from the right side and on the inside.

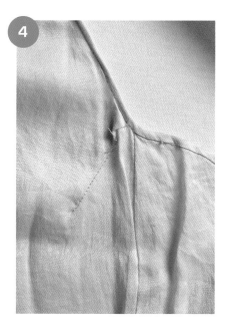

Bodice dart detail.

Bodice and trouser joined at the centre front.

Seam detail at the crotch, on the inside.

Attaching the binding around the bodice

The raw edges of the bodice around the sides and back are finished using a self-fabric binding. This type of finishing detail gives a real couture feel to the garment. Begin by cutting two strips of the dress fabric on the bias and measuring approximately 38–41.5cm (15–16in) in length (this allows for turnings) and 2.8cm (1⅛in) wide. This width should be sufficient to create a 0.3cm (⅛in) finished binding. For the best possible finish, ensure the fabric strips are cut on the true bias and follow each step carefully.

(9) To create the binding, start by machine stitching a straight stay-stitch along the raw edges of the bodice to reduce the likelihood of the fabric stretching whilst the binding is applied. Make the stitch line 0.3cm (⅛in) in from the raw edge. Next, with

right sides of the fabric together, position the binding strip along the bodice edge, aligning the raw edges. Gently stretch the binding strip as it is being positioned onto the bodice to ensure the curve is neat and tight. It is advisable to tack the binding strip onto the bodice before stitching, using the stay-stitching as a guide.

(10) Stitch the binding strip into position, just outside the tacking/stay-stitch line. Once each strip is stitched, carefully and gently press the binding up toward the raw edge using the tip of the iron. This will help create a smooth seam edge.

The next stages are worked from the inside of the bodice. Begin by taking the remaining raw edge of the binding and fold it in half so that the raw edge sits behind the seam allowance and touches the seam. Next, fold it in half again, so the top fold touches the seam stitches, and secure this edge along the stitching line by hand, using a slip-stitch. Carefully press the finished binding to create a sharp edge.

Creating the centre back placket

(11) Begin by cutting two strips of fabric on the straight grain, one measuring 16cm (6¼in) long x 4cm (1½in) wide for the left-hand opening and 16cm (6¼in) long x 1.8cm (¾in) wide for the right-hand opening. Starting with the left-hand side of the opening, take the wider strip and, with right sides together, align the strip along the raw edge of the opening and stitch a 0.7cm (¼in) seam down to the top of the centre back trouser seam. Press the fabric strip toward the centre back, then fold under to create a 1.5cm (⅝in) placket.

(12) Fold over the top and bottom edges of the placket strip to neaten off and press. This edge can be secured by hand using a slip-stitch.

(13) Next, and working on the inside of the trouser opening, turn under the remaining raw edge of the placket strip, so that the folded edge lines up with the seam stitching.

(14) Tack into place, then machine top-stitch into place, directly over the seam.

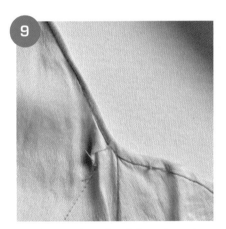

Bodice binding detail, from the right side.

Detail of binding, inside finishing.

Left placket detail, from the right side.

Detail of the placket ends, from the inside.

(15) Now create the right-hand side of the placket by taking the remaining narrow fabric strip and, with right sides together, align the strip along the raw edge of the opening and stitch in the same manner as the left-hand side. Once stitched, fold the strip to the inside of the opening and press along

Left placket detail, on the inside.

Left placket top-stitching detail.

Right placket detail, from the inside.

Right placket detail, from the right side.

Placket attachment at the waist.

Hook and bar detail on the placket.

the seam edge to create the placket facing.

(16) Working on the inside of the trousers, turn the facing under approximately 0.3cm (⅛in) and press to create a sharp edge.

(17) On the original garment, the placket facing is only attached at the waist seam with a few hand-stitches.

(18) The bottom edge of the placket facing can be finished in the same manner as the left-hand side. For the top edge, simply turn under and press to neaten, as this will be finished when the shoulder straps are attached. Finally, apply the hooks and bars to the placket. Start by placing the five hooks along the right-hand placket facing, on the inside of the trouser, spacing evenly. Only stitch onto the facing and not through all the layers. This will give a neat appearance on the right side. Utilize the seam allowance layers to stitch through and secure the hook head. Stitch the bars onto the left-hand placket in positions corresponding to the hooks and following down the top-stitched seam.

Making up and attaching the shoulder straps

(19) Take the shoulder strap pattern piece and begin by folding it in half lengthways as indicated on the pattern. With right sides together, stitch to the marks indicated on the pattern using a 0.7cm (¼in) seam. Once stitched, turn right sides out and carefully press along the seams so they sit along the edges. Snip into the seam allowance at the points where they meet the central neckline.

(20) The next step is to attach the strap to the bodice neckline. Take the turned-out strap and, with right sides together, position it onto the neckline, aligning both centre front points. Ease the neckline onto the strap and then stitch into place using a 0.7cm (¼in) seam allowance. Press the seam upwards so that the strap now becomes the neckline.

(21) Working on the inside of the neckline, turn under the remaining raw edge of the strap, lining up the folded edge with the seamline. Secure by hand using a slip-stitch.

(22) Next, pleat each end of the shoulder strap to the marks indicated on the pattern and press the pleats approximately 5cm (2in) along their length to set.

(23) Trim the edges and finish by hand-sewing through all the layers using an overcast stitch.

Neckline detail, from the right side

Neckline detail, on the inside.

Pleats on the shoulder straps, detail.

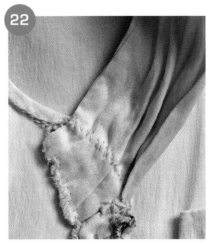

Pleats on the shoulder straps, stitching on the inside.

Shoulder straps position, centre back, from the right side.

Shoulder strap stitching, detail, on the inside.

Centre front detail, on the inside.

Detail of the neckline bow gathers on the left hand side.

(24) Attach each strap onto the back bodice, aligning the folded edge of the strap with the centre back edge of the bodice and with the top edge of the bodice binding placed 1.8cm (¾in) up from the bottom edge of the strap.
(25) Stitch the strap to the bodice by hand, through the top edge of the binding and through all the layers,

using a slip-stitch.
(26) Finally, gather the shoulder strap at the centre front neck to a measurement of 2.5cm (1in), in preparation for the attachment of the bow. This can be carried out by machine or hand-stitching.

Making up and attaching the neck bow
To create the neck bow, start by folding the pattern piece in half lengthways, as indicated on the pattern. With right sides together, stitch along the edges and across the two ends to the marks indicated on the pattern, leaving an opening to turn out the bow. Trim the seam allowance to 0.3cm (⅛in), snipping across the corners to reduce bulk. Turn the piece right sides out, taking care to ensure the corners are sharp. Press flat, turning under the unstitched sections of the bow to align with the stitched seam. Hand-sew it closed, using a slip-stitch.
(27) Next, the knot will need to be tied. Lay the bow flat with the folded edge at the top and, starting at the left-hand side, gather the fabric section together, approximately 11−11.5 cm (4¼ −4½in) from the left-hand edge and hold loosely. Take the remainder of the fabric and tie a knot close to the held gathers, slowly tightening and manipulating the knot so the flat side is uppermost and lies centrally.

Knot detail on the neckline bow.

Neckline bow in position.

Bow attachment at the neckline, detail.

(28) Position the tied bow onto the centre front neck band, aligning the knot with the central gathers on the band. Check that the bow is centralized and hand-sew onto the neckband, just beneath the knot, to conceal the stitches. Take care to stitch through all the layers to secure.
(29) Finally, secure the top edge of each bow end, approximately 1.5cm (⅝in) in from the end.

Making up the waist sash and belt loops
(30) To create the waist sash, start by folding the pattern piece in half lengthways, as indicated on the pattern. With right sides together, stitch

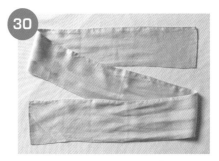

Waist sash completed.

round the two ends and the long edge to the marks indicated on the pattern; this will leave an opening for turning out the sash. Trim the seam allowance to 0.3cm (⅛in), snipping across the corners to reduce bulk. Turn the sash right side out, taking care to ensure the corners are sharp. Press flat, turning under the unstitched sections of the sash to align with the stitched seam.

Hand-sew closed, using a slip-stitch.

To create the belt loops, first cut two sections of fabric on the straight grain, measuring approximately 7cm x 2.5cm (¾ x 1in). Next, with the right side facing down, fold each long edge into the centre of the fabric strip and press to create sharp edges. With the raw edges inside the strip, fold it in half again lengthways and join the two

folded edges together using a slip-stitch.

(31) Press the prepared loop sections and turn each end under 0.7cm (¼in). Position each loop at the side seams, measuring equally either side of the waist seam. Attach the belt loops to the playsuit by hand using a slip-stitch and ensuring all the layers are secured.

31

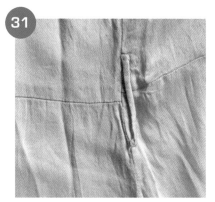

Belt loop attachment at the waistline.

STYLE GUIDE

This elegant and simple playsuit would make a beautiful evening outfit, given its low back and the silky wide-leg trouser. The minimal decorative bow and tie waist would suggest that you add distinctive but equally minimal accessories to dress this playsuit up. The soft and lightweight fabric would also make this garment an ideal summer outfit; however, you might opt for a heavier richer fabric for either an autumnal outfit or a dressier evening ensemble. The luxurious nature of a velvet would make this a wonderful party look, perhaps topped with a classic leather jacket for the contemporary wearer.

In a light fabric this playsuit could also be worn as a cover-up, perhaps an outfit you would wear when travelling to a beach or pool with your swimwear worn underneath.

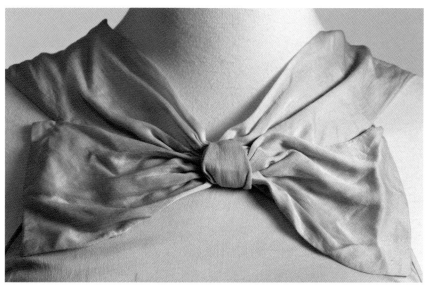

Bow detail of green silk playsuit.

Back detail of green silk playsuit.

Front detail of green silk playsuit.

PLAYSUIT
SCALE 1:2 FOR ALL PATTERN PIECES ON THIS PAGE

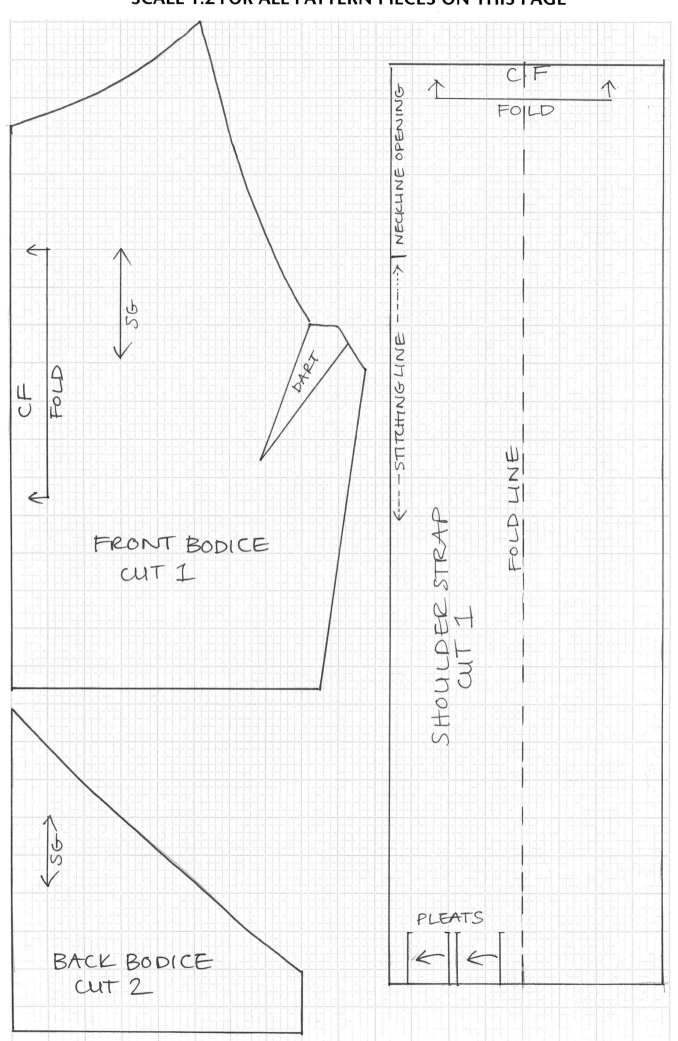

FRONT BODICE
CUT 1

SG

CF
FOLD

DART

BACK BODICE
CUT 2

SG

C F
FOLD

NECKLINE OPENING

STITCHING LINE

SHOULDER STRAP
CUT 1

FOLD LINE

PLEATS

PLAYSUIT
SCALE 1:5 FOR ALL PATTERN PIECES ON THIS PAGE

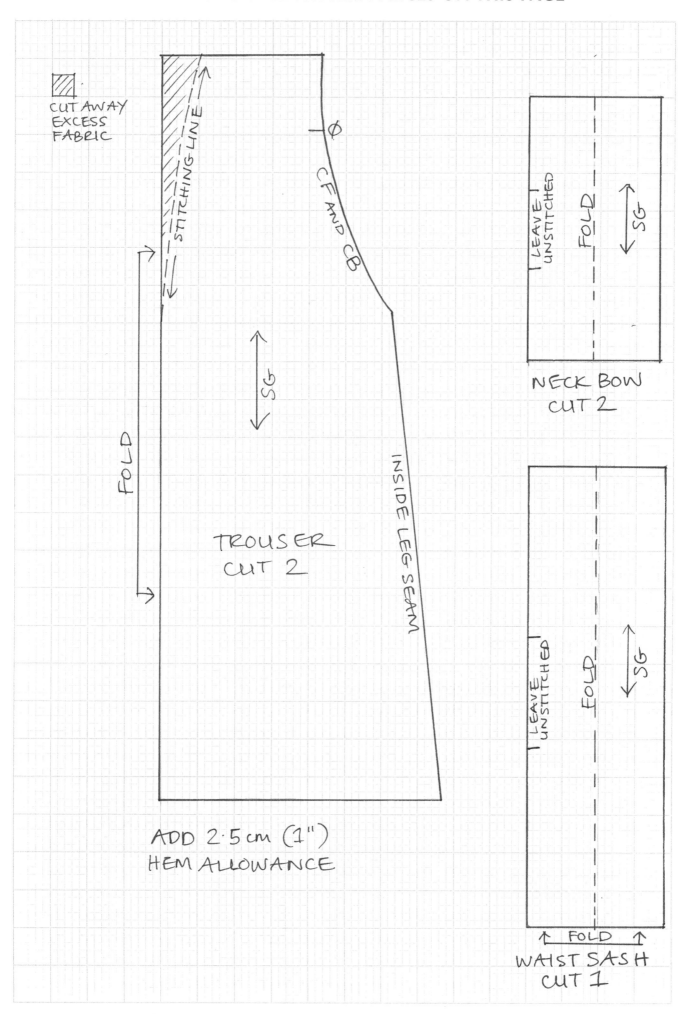

CUT AWAY EXCESS FABRIC

STITCHING LINE

CF AND CB

Ø

FOLD

SG

INSIDE LEG SEAM

TROUSER
CUT 2

ADD 2·5 cm (1") HEM ALLOWANCE

LEAVE UNSTITCHED

FOLD

SG

NECK BOW
CUT 2

LEAVE UNSTITCHED

FOLD

SG

FOLD

WAIST SASH
CUT 1

Summer Day Dress

7

This pretty, lightweight day dress is a very flattering style with a delicate floral sprig motif design over the pale yellow polyester semi-sheer fabric. The dress is unlined and has no fastenings and the full-length skirt is cut on the bias grain to allow stretch and movement. The bodice is cut on the straight grain and is loose-fitting, cinching in at the waist with belt ties. The waistline curves up to a point at the centre front bust.

The short, cap sleeves are gathered onto the armhole, creating a frilled effect, and are bound in a bold yellow cotton bias binding. This contrasting finish is continued at the simple V-neck. The sleeve and neckline binding would work equally well with any complementary or contrasting colour; for a hint of sophistication, a satin binding could be used.

The dress would originally have been worn with an under-slip, but could be made in a less sheer fabric if desired; any light, soft fabric that drapes well would be suitable. The dress uses a combination of French seams and hand-finished seams using a blanket stitch.

Note: Due to the cut of the dress, it is not suitable for very narrow-width fabrics; however, the pattern pages show where extra widths could be joined, should the need arise.

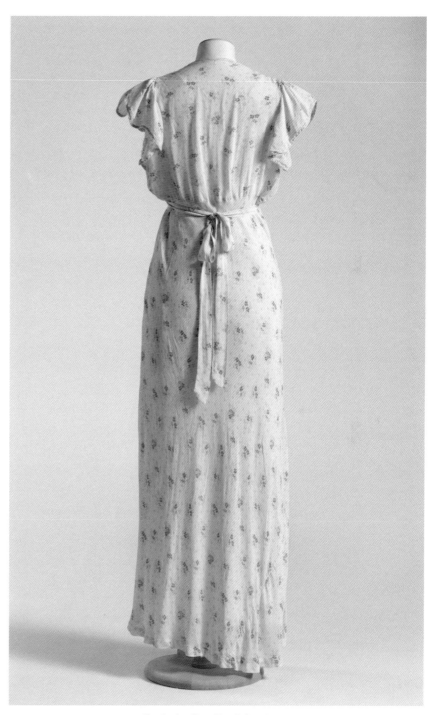

Back of yellow floral day dress.

Left: Yellow floral day dress.

Instructions for Making Up the Dress

To start

Begin by cutting out all the pattern pieces for the dress, adding seam and hem allowances, and set them aside.

Making up the bodice

(1) Start by applying the bias binding to the necklines of the front and back bodice sections. Cut two lengths of bias binding measuring 38cm (15in) for the front bodice and 20.5cm (8in) for the back bodice. With right sides together, position each around the corresponding neckline, lining up the raw edges. Take time to do this and gently stretch the binding around any curved areas to ensure a smooth line. Stitch into position following the fold line of the binding as the seam allowance. Once attached and using

FABRIC SUGGESTIONS AND NOTIONS

Any semi-sheer synthetic or natural fabric would suit this dress to complement its summery styling. Polyesters, cottons and cotton mixes, georgette and (if a high-quality finish is desired) lightweight silks could be considered. Patterned fabrics would work better than plain and provide a great opportunity to get creative with colour and design.

Matching sewing thread

Approximately 1.43m (56in) of 1.2cm (½in) width bias binding

5 STEPS TO CREATE A 1930s SUMMER DAY DRESS

1. Cut out all the pattern pieces

2. Make up the bodice

3. Prepare and attach the cap sleeves

4. Make up and attach the skirt

5. Make up and attach the belt ties

Neckline binding completed.

Neckline binding detail, from the right side.

Neckline binding detail, from the inside.

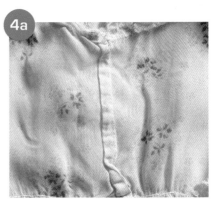

French seam detail at side seam, from the inside.

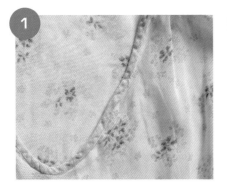

French seam detail at shoulder, from the inside.

MEASUREMENTS

Bust: 91.5cm (36in)

Waist: 76cm (30in)

Hips: 96.5cm (38in)

Approximate dress size: UK 10/12, US 6/8, EU 38/40

the tip of the iron, carefully press the binding up toward the edge of the neckline.

(2) Next, fold the binding over to the wrong side of the fabric (the inside of the bodice) so that the free pre-turned edge meets the seamline and secure by hand using a slip-stitch.

(3) Press carefully to finish the completed binding and create a crisp edge.

(4) The front and back bodice sections can now be joined at the sides and shoulders using French seams. Start creating this twice-stitched seam by placing the wrong sides of the fabric together and then proceed to stitch the seam in the usual manner, after which the seam is pressed open. Next, trim both raw edges of the seam allowance to approximately 1cm (⅜in) in width, ready to complete the second stage. This will ensure that no fibres protrude from the finished French seam on the right side of the fabric.

The second stage in creating the seam is to fold the fabric back on itself, so the right sides are now facing one another and the raw edges of the first seam are completely enclosed. Stitch a 0.7cm (¼in) wide seam and finish by pressing the seam toward the back of the garment.

Preparing and attaching the cap sleeves

(5) Start by taking each sleeve pattern piece and gather or pleat the straight edge between the marks indicated on the pattern by Ø and to a finished measurement of 25cm (10in). Make sure the fullness is concentrated around the shoulder and gently decreases toward the points at either end of the sleeve.

(6) Next, apply bias binding to the curved edge of each sleeve. Cut two lengths of bias binding to a measurement of 81–84cm (32–33in) which allows for turnings and follow the instructions as explained in Steps 1, 2 and 3 (Making up the bodice).

(7) Take the completed cap sleeves and, with right sides together, align the centre point of each sleeve with the shoulder seam and continue to position each side of the sleeves around the armholes, finishing at the bodice side seam. Finish here by bringing together the two pointed ends to cross over at the underarm.

Cap sleeve gathers, from the right side.

Cap sleeve binding complete, from the right side.

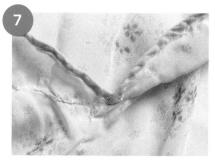

Binding finish at the underarm, detail.

Cap sleeve inserted, from the right side.

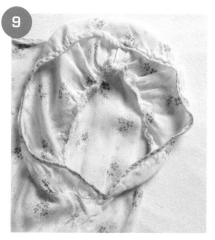

Finish detail inside cap sleeve.

(8) Stitch the sleeves into position and press the seam allowances in toward the bodice.

(9) Trim the seam allowance and neaten by hand using either a blanket stitch, as in the original dress, or (if preferred) an overcast stitch. Make sure all the fabric layers are secured.

Making up and attaching the skirt

(10) If using a narrower fabric, begin by attaching the corner sections to both front and back skirt panels as indicated on the pattern. With right sides together, join the sections, then trim the seam allowance and finish by hand using either a blanket stitch, as in the original dress, or (if preferred) an overcast stitch.

(11) Join the front and back skirt panels together using French seams, as described in Step 4 (Making up the bodice). Take extra care not to overstretch the seams, as the skirt is cut on the bias grain. Next, fold under a 0.7cm (¼in) turning at the skirt waistline and press to create a crisp, sharp edge, taking extra care to ensure the point is sharp at the centre front. The seam allowance at the centre front can be clipped at this stage to reduce

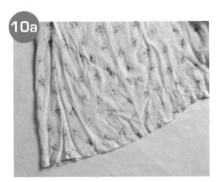

Additional skirt section attached, from the right side

Additional skirt section, finish detail, from the inside.

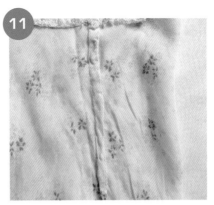

French seams at the side seam, from the inside.

Front bodice attached to the skirt, from the right side.

Back bodice attached to the skirt, from the right side.

bulk.

(12) With right sides uppermost, take the assembled skirt and position it onto the waistline of the bodice with the folded edge of the skirt waistline placed 0.7cm (¼in) up from the raw

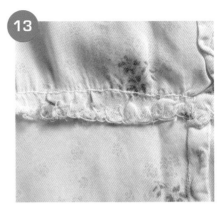

Waistline finish, detail, on the inside.

Skirt hem finish, detail.

edge of the bodice. Align the side seams, centre front and centre back points and then ease the remaining bodice fabric onto the skirt, ensuring that any small pleats are evenly spaced. At this point it is advisable to tack the bodice and skirt together in preparation for stitching. From the right side, machine edge-stitch the skirt and bodice, securing all the layers.

(13) Trim the seam allowance and finish by hand using either a blanket stitch, as in the original dress, or (if preferred) an overcast stitch. Press to finish.

(14) To complete the skirt, finish by turning under a double 1.8cm (¾in) hem, taking care not to overstretch the fabric, and ease in where necessary. It may be beneficial to tack the hem into place before securing to the skirt, using a slip-stitch. Press to finish.

Making up and attaching the belt ties

(15) Begin by taking both pattern pieces and fold them in half lengthways so the right sides are inside. Stitch along the entire length of each tie, using a 0.7cm (¼in) seam and leaving both ends of the ties unstitched. When stitching, leave a substantial length of sewing thread at one end, to assist with turning it through. Trim the seam allowance to 0.3cm (⅛in) on each belt tie and turn through. Press the ties flat, with the seamline positioned along one edge.

At each straight and angled end, turn in the seam allowances and secure by hand using a slip-stitch. Press to finish.

(16) Attach the completed belt ties to the centre front waist at the marks indicated on the pattern. Start by placing the straight end of each tie into position, with the angled ends facing toward the centre front, and secure through all the layers by hand, using a close back-stitch. The free edge can then be secured by hand using a slip-stitch.

(17) Finish by carefully pressing the belt ties over at the joins to now face toward the back of the dress.

Belt tie angled end, detail.

Belt ties attached to the dress.

Belt tie position on the bodice.

Detail of yellow floral day dress.

Back detail of yellow floral day dress.

(17) 114 Belt tie stitching detail, from the right side.

SUMMER DAY DRESS
SCALE 1:5 FOR ALL PATTERN PIECES ON THIS PAGE

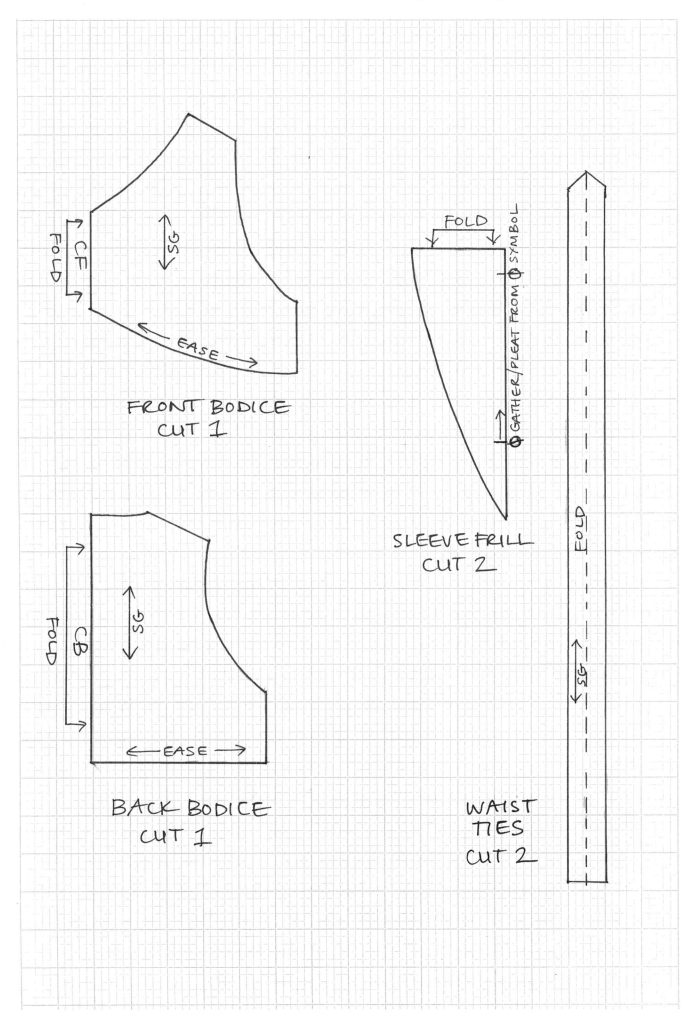

FRONT BODICE
CUT 1

BACK BODICE
CUT 1

SLEEVE FRILL
CUT 2

WAIST
TIES
CUT 2

SUMMER DAY DRESS
SCALE 1:10 FOR ALL PATTERN PIECES ON THIS PAGE

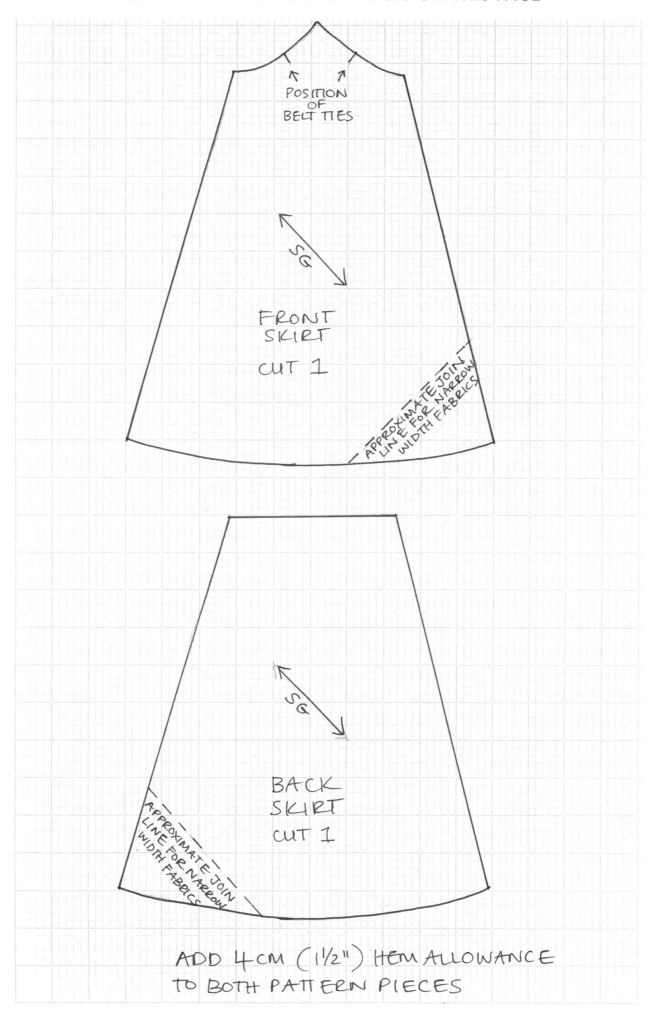

POSITION OF BELT TIES

SG

FRONT SKIRT

CUT 1

APPROXIMATE JOIN LINE FOR NARROW WIDTH FABRICS

SG

BACK SKIRT

CUT 1

APPROXIMATE JOIN LINE FOR NARROW WIDTH FABRICS

ADD 4 CM (1½") HEM ALLOWANCE TO BOTH PATTERN PIECES

Long-Sleeved Day Dress

8

This sophisticated day dress in bottle green stretch crêpe has an all-over pattern of muted yellow and green floral sprigs, complemented by a stylized geometric floral pattern. The soft yet structured styling of the dress incorporates a loose-fitting bodice with panelled skirt, long sleeves and flamboyant, circular-cut neck frill.

The softly scooped V neck is finished with a self-fabric binding. The blouson-style sleeves taper toward the wrist with deep, top-stitched pleats and are simply finished at the cuff with a self-fabric binding that echoes the neckline. The panelled skirt falls below the knee and the dress fastens at the left with a placket opening secured with press studs. The dress is unlined, with all seams finished by hand using an overcast stitch.

The belt loops at the waist indicate that the dress would have originally had a belt to cinch it in and this would probably have been made from the dress fabric.

Back of green long-sleeved day dress.

Left: Green long-sleeved day dress.

Instructions for Making Up the Dress

To start
Begin by cutting out all the pattern pieces for the dress, adding seam and hem allowances, and set them aside.

Making up the bodice
(1) Take the front and back bodice sections and, with right sides together, stitch the shoulder and side seams, ensuring the left-hand side seam is joined only as far as the marks indicated on the pattern (this will

Bodice seam finish on the inside.

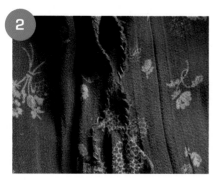

Left side bodice seam, from the inside.

create the side opening). On both the shoulder seams and right-hand side seam, trim the seam allowance and finish by hand using an overcast stitch, securing all the layers. Press the seams toward the centre back of the dress.

(2) The left-hand side seam is pressed open. Trim the raw edges and finish by hand on each side, using an overcast stitch.

Making up and inserting the sleeves
(3) Begin by creating the pleats at the wrist on each sleeve section. Fold the pleats toward the centre of the sleeve as indicated on the pattern and top-stitch to secure through all the layers, 0.7cm (¼in) in from the folded edges of the pleats. Stitch up one side from the wrist, then across both pleats and down the other side, back toward the wrist.

(4) There will be a significant amount of fabric left inside the sleeve; this should not be cut away. Excess at the base of the pleats can be tacked across the wrist to hold it in place, making sure that it is lined up at the raw edges and the pleats lie smoothly inside the sleeve. Press to finish.

(5) The next stage is to apply a binding along the bottom edge of the wrist. Start by cutting two strips of the dress fabric on the bias grain, measuring 23cm (9in) long (this allows for turnings) x 2.8cm (1⅛in) wide. This width should be sufficient to create a 0.3cm (⅛in) finished binding. For the

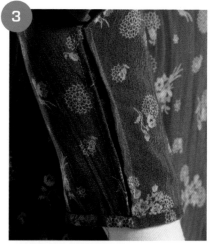

Sleeve pleat top-stitching, detail, from the right side.

Sleeve pleats, detail, from the inside.

best possible finish, ensure the fabric strips are cut on the true bias and follow each step carefully.

To create the binding, start by machine stitching a straight stay-stitch around the raw edges at the wrist to reduce the likelihood of the fabric stretching whilst the binding is applied. Position the stitch line 0.3cm (⅛in) in from the raw edge. Next, with right sides of the fabric together, position the binding strip along the wrist edge, aligning the raw edges. Gently stretch the binding strip as it is being positioned onto the sleeve to ensure the line is neat and tight. It is advisable to tack the binding strip onto the sleeve before stitching, using the stay-stitching as a guide.

Stitch the binding strip into position, just outside the tacking/stay-stitch line. Once each strip is stitched, carefully and gently press the binding up toward the raw edge using the tip of the iron. This will help create a smooth seam edge. The next stages are worked from the inside of the sleeve.

Begin by taking the remaining raw edge of the binding and fold in half so that the raw edge sits behind the seam allowance and touches the seam. Next,

Binding at the wrist edge, detail, from the right side.

Sleeve seam detail, on the inside.

Sleeve side opening, from the right side.

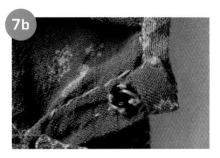

Sleeve side opening, detail.

Sleeve binding detail at the wrist opening, from the inside.

fold in half again, so the top fold touches the seam stitches and secure this edge along the stitching line by hand, using a slip-stitch. Carefully press the finished binding to create a sharp edge.

(6) Once the binding has been applied, the sleeves can be made up. With right sides together, join each sleeve seam as far as the marks indicated on the pattern, which will leave a small 4cm (1½in) opening at the wrist.

(7) Do not trim the seam allowance; finish the seams up to the wrist opening by hand, using an overcast stitch and securing all the layers.

(8) To complete the wrist opening, start by turning under the back section of

the opening and secure by hand using a slip-stitch. The front section of the opening is simply finished by applying a small section of binding to the raw edge, using the method previously described for the wrist edge finishing.

(9) Complete the opening by attaching a press stud to close. Position the stud just below the binding or, if using a particularly soft or lightweight fabric, the stud can be attached to the binding for more durability.

(10) The next step is to insert the sleeves into the bodice armholes. Begin

Press stud fastenings at the wrist opening, detail.

Sleeve head gathers, from the inside.

Armhole seam completed, from the inside.

by gathering or pleating the sleeve head between the marks indicated on the pattern and to a finished measurement of approximately 15.5cm (6in). Make sure the fullness of any gathering is concentrated around the shoulder.

(11) With right sides together, position the sleeve within the armhole, aligning the central point of the sleeve head with the shoulders and the sleeve seam and bodice side seams. Ease the remainder of the sleeve into the armhole, stitch into place, then trim the allowance and finish by hand using an overcast stitch, securing all the layers. Carefully press the seam back toward the inside of the sleeve to finish.

Attaching the neckline frill and applying the binding

(12) Begin by hemming the outer curved edges and the straight centre back ends of the frill pattern pieces. Roll a 0.3cm (⅛in) hem over twice and hand-sew using a small, neat slip-stitch. Press to finish.

(13) With right sides together, join the two frill sections from the front points and along the seamline indicated on the pattern. Stitch, then trim the seam allowance down to 0.3cm (⅛in) and finish by hand using an overcast stitch, securing both layers. Press the seam to

one side to finish.

(14) The neck frill can now be attached to the bodice neckline. With right sides uppermost, position the unfinished, small curved edge onto the neckline, ensuring that the centre front seam is in line with the centre front point of the neckline.

(15) The two centre back ends of the frill come together at the centre back of the neckline. Make sure the raw edges of both frill and neckline are aligned and gently stretch the frill edge as necessary to fit smoothly around the neckline.

(16) Join the two, using a machine stay-stitch, approximately 0.3cm (⅛in) down from the raw edge. This stitch will ensure the neckline is not overstretched when applying the binding. Apply a self-fabric binding, employing the method described in Step 5 (Making up and inserting the

Neck frill hem detail, from the right side.

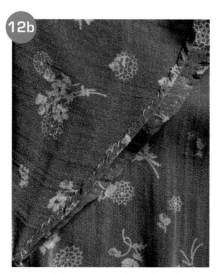

Neck frill hem detail, underside.

sleeves) and using a strip of the dress fabric, cut on the bias grain, measuring 58.5cm (23in) long x 2.8cm (1⅛in) wide. The neckline binding starts and

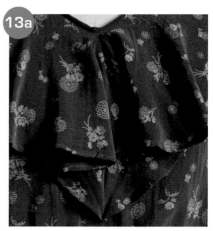

Centre seam of the neck frill, from the right side.

Centre seam finish of the neck frill, underside.

Neck frill at the centre front, detail.

Neck frill at the centre back, detail.

Binding at the centre front neckline, detail.

Neckline binding completed.

Front skirt panel, from the right side.

Back skirt panel, from the right side.

ends at the centre front, joining at the V point, with one end turned under to neaten. Once complete, press to finish.

Making up the skirt

(17) Begin by making up the front skirt section. With right sides together, stitch two of the side skirt panels onto the centre front panel. Repeat the process for the back skirt panel using the remaining pattern pieces.

(18) Trim all the seam allowances and finish by hand using an overcast stitch, securing all the layers. Press the seams toward the direction of the side seams.

(19) With right sides together, join the skirt panels at the side seams, stitching the left seam to the marks indicated on the pattern and leaving an opening of 10cm (4in). Finish the seams by hand, using an overcast stitch, securing all the layers. Finish the left seam only to the base of the opening and then press the seams toward the centre back.

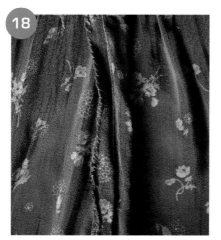

Skirt seam finish on the inside, detail.

Finish at the left side seam, detail.

Joining the skirt and bodice

(20) With right sides together, join the skirt to the bodice, aligning the side seams, centre front and centre back points. The bodice will require easing into place along the skirt waistline and it may be necessary to form small, even pleats to achieve this.

(21) Stitch the bodice and skirt together and trim the seam allowance to approximately 0.7cm (¼in). Finish by hand, using an overcast stitch to secure all the layers. Press the finished seam allowance up toward the bodice.

Creating the side opening

(22) Start by preparing the front placket side of the opening. Cut a section of the dress fabric on the straight grain and measuring 20cm (8in) long x 3cm (1¼in) wide. In the original dress the placket strip was cut with the fabric selvedge running along one long side and this avoided the need to finish or hem that edge.

(23) With right sides together, join the strip to the front side of the opening on the dress, aligning the raw edges. (If the strip has been cut with a selvedge at one side, do not use this side for the seam join.) Stitch into position, trim the seam allowance, turn the strip to the

Back edge of the side placket, detail, from the inside.

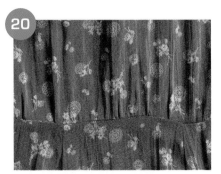

Centre front bodice waistline ease, from the right side.

Side placket, front section, from the right side.

Placket stitching, detail, from the right side.

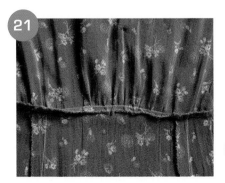

Seam finish at the waistline, on the inside.

Waist attachment inside the front placket, detail.

inside of the dress to just beyond the seam line and press to create a defined edge to the front placket.

(24) To secure the placket turning into position, stitch it to the waistline seam by hand, using a back-stitch.

(25) Next, prepare the back placket. Cut a strip of dress fabric measuring 20cm (8in) long x 3cm (1¼in) wide and join it to the dress opening in the same manner as the front placket. To complete the placket on this side, turn under the fabric strip on the double, to essentially create a 1cm (⅜in) binding.

(26) Press, then stitch through all the layers by hand, using a back-stitch. Finally, attach the press stud fastenings, positioning them evenly along the placket, and sew into place.

Finishing the skirt hem

(27) The skirt on the original dress has a deep hem, which suggests it may have been previously altered. For a neater and less heavy hem, the pattern in this book has been adapted to allow for a 4cm (1½in) finished hem. Begin by folding under a 1.2cm (½in) turning and press lightly to create a soft, folded edge. Turn the fabric under again to a

Skirt hem finish, from the right side and the inside.

measurement of 4cm (1½in) and tack into place. Working from the inside, secure the hem to the skirt by hand, using a slip-stitch, and press to finish.

Creating a belt

If a belt is to be made, its length depends upon whether a classic buckled or a sash-style belt is desired. If the former, an early plastic vintage buckle would set the dress off and give a smart, polished look to the garment. For the latter, a simple turned-through strip of the dress fabric, measuring approximately 2.5–4 cm (1–1½in) finished width with straight ends, would suffice.

Belt loops, from the right side.

(28) The belt loops are simply made by turning through strips of the dress fabric to a finished measurement of 5cm (2in) long (without turnings) x 0.7cm (¼in) wide. Attach to the dress by hand, using a slip-stitch, positioning the loops at the side waist, half above the waistline seam, half below.

Close-up detail of the placket, from the inside.

STYLE GUIDE

This long-sleeved day dress could be utilized as a sophisticated work outfit, worn with some simple jewellery to modernize it, and even pairing it with a leather belt. You might also decide to make this dress in a heavier fabric such as a denim, to create a contemporary denim shirt dress. The ruffled edging on the collar would work really well in a deep blue lightweight denim, as would the ability to belt the dress at the waist. This dress is a really versatile length that would suit both summer and winter, worn with thick or thin tights, and some simple leather ankle boots.

Neck frill on green long-sleeved day dress.

Cuff detail on green long-sleeved day dress.

Side view of green long-sleeved day dress.

LONG-SLEEVED DAY DRESS
SCALE 1:5 FOR ALL PATTERN PIECES ON THIS PAGE

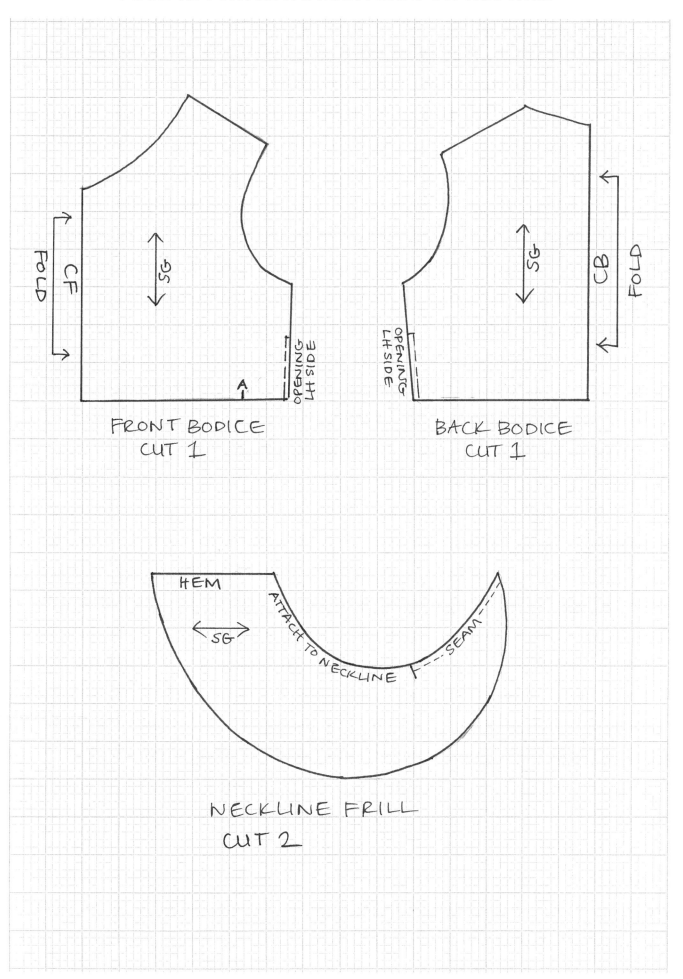

FOLD

CF

SG

OPENING LH SIDE

A

FRONT BODICE
CUT 1

SG

CB

FOLD

OPENING LH SIDE

BACK BODICE
CUT 1

HEM

SG

ATTACH TO NECKLINE

SEAM

NECKLINE FRILL
CUT 2

LONG-SLEEVED DAY DRESS
SCALE 1:5 FOR ALL PATTERN PIECES ON THIS PAGE

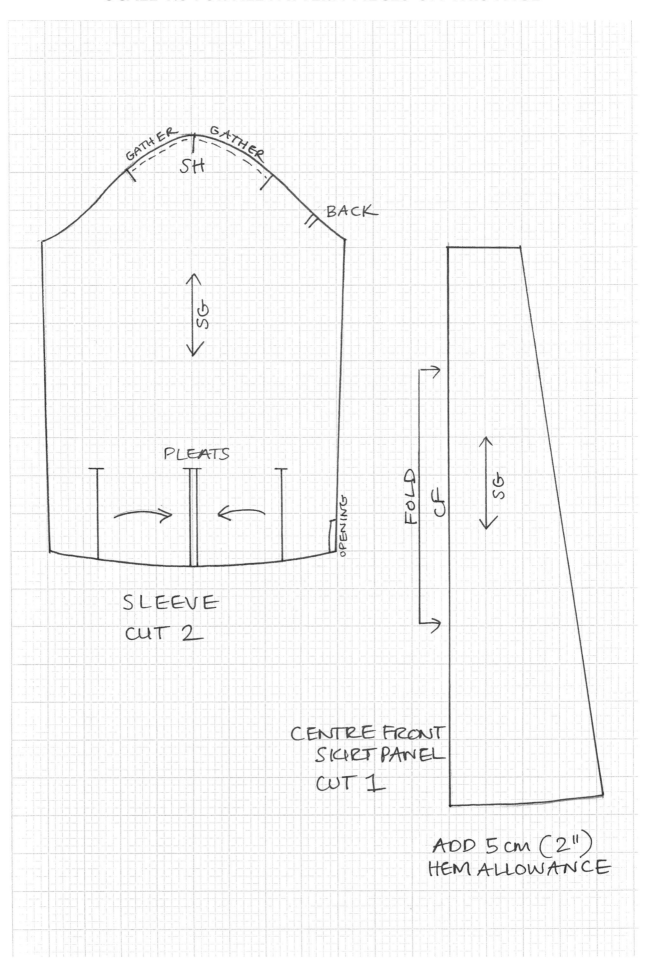

GATHER SH GATHER

BACK

SG

PLEATS

SLEEVE
CUT 2

OPENING

FOLD CF

SG

CENTRE FRONT
SKIRT PANEL
CUT 1

ADD 5 cm (2")
HEM ALLOWANCE

LONG-SLEEVED DAY DRESS
SCALE 1:5 FOR ALL PATTERN PIECES ON THIS PAGE

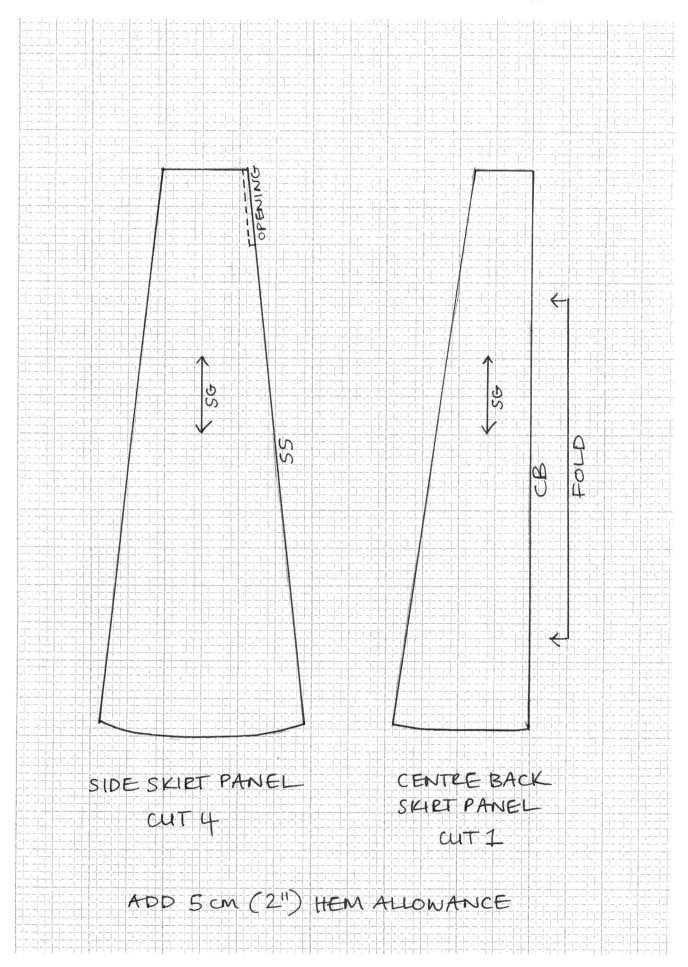

SIDE SKIRT PANEL
CUT 4

CENTRE BACK
SKIRT PANEL
CUT 1

ADD 5 cm (2") HEM ALLOWANCE

Tailored Dress and Matching Cape

This smart and sophisticated dress and matching shoulder cape are constructed in a muted green, satin-backed crêpe and have structured shaping using pleated panels to create the sharp silhouette. This is enhanced by the use of machined edge-stitching detail on the pleated dress panels and the cape seams.

The skirt pleats on the dress fall from the knee and give fullness and movement to the lower skirt. The dress has short sleeves, which are shaped at the sleeve head using darts and are pleated at the sleeve hem in continuation of the tailored appearance of the garment. A simple, fold-down collar softens the neckline and the back neck closure fastens using covered buttons and hand-worked loops. The dress is unlined and fastens at the left side with a hook and press stud placket.

The waist-length cape is a boxy shape with deep, solid shoulder pads that give a square-shouldered appearance to the garment, reflecting the structured look of the dress. The cape is an edge-to-edge design at the centre front, fastening at the neck with a single hook and hand-worked bar. The cape's side panels are pleated and machine top-stitched at the head to give the illusion of a sleeve and they also add fullness and swing from the shoulder. The cape is unlined.

The inside seams are either left with selvedges intact, trimmed using pinking shears or finished by hand using overcast and herringbone stitches.

Green tailored dress and matching cape.

Left: Green tailored dress.

Instructions for Making Up the Dress and Cape

To start
Begin by cutting out all the pattern pieces for the dress and cape, adding seam and hem allowances, and set them aside.

Making Up the Dress
Joining the centre front and side front panels
(1) Take the two side dress panels and, with right sides together, join to the centre front panel. Stitch and press the seams open. Trim the non-selvedge side of the seam to 0.7cm (¼in) and finish by hand using an overcast stitch.
(2) Begin by stitching the bust darts

Seam at the base of the centre front skirt, from the inside.

MEASUREMENTS

Bust: 74.5/76cm (29/30in)

Waist: 71cm (28in)

Hips: 86.5cm (34in)

Approximate dress size: UK 8/10, US 4/6, EU 36/38

FABRIC SUGGESTIONS AND NOTIONS

Mediumweight fabrics are ideal for this outfit and therefore crêpes and fine wools or wool mixes would work well. Due to the unusual cut it is advisable to avoid fabric patterns that require aligning, such as stripes or tartans/checks.

6 x 1.2cm (½in) covered buttons

3 x 1cm (⅜in) metal hooks (dress)

1 x 0.7cm (¼in) metal hook (cape)

3 x 0.7cm (¼in) press studs

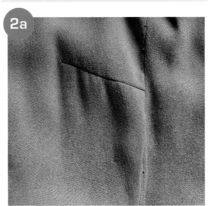

Bodice dart, from the right side.

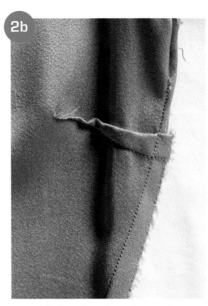

Bodice dart, from the inside.

17 STEPS TO CREATE A 1930s TAILORED DRESS WITH MATCHING CAPE

Dress:

1. Cut out all the pattern pieces

2. Join the centre front and side front panels

3. Prepare the front panel pleat

4. Join the centre back panels

5. Prepare the centre back panel pleats

6. Trim the front and back panel pleats

7. Join the front and back panels

8. Create the side placket closure

9. Prepare and insert the sleeves

10. Prepare and attach the collar

11. Finish the centre back neck opening

12. Finish the skirt hem

Cape:

13. Prepare the centre back panel and pleat insert

14. Join the shoulder seams

15. Create and insert the side panels and shoulder pads

16. Create neckline and centre front facings

17. Finish the cape hem

and pressing them up toward the armholes.
(3) Working from the right side, fold the pleats marked B, C and D on the pattern toward the centre front as indicated and tack into position from the shoulders down to the bottom of the hem. Press the pleats into position, then machine edge-stitch from the

shoulders down to the marks indicated on the pattern. Press again along the entire length of the pleats and remove the tacking stitches. To keep the lower skirt pleats in place it is a good idea to secure them temporarily by running a tacking stitch across the base of the hemline.

Preparing the front panel pleat

Now the centre front pleat, marked A on the pattern, can be prepared. Begin by cutting away the excess fabric at the

Edge-stitching on the dress front, from the right side.

Centre front bodice, from the inside.

Centre front bodice, edge-stitching detail.

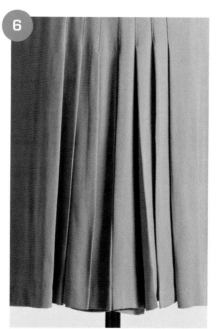

Skirt pleats at the centre front, from the right side.

centre front bodice as indicated on the pattern, leaving an allowance of 1.2cm (½in). Clip into the allowance diagonally at the point where the vertical and horizontal raw edges meet, then turn under the seam allowance either side of the centre front line, from the neckline to the waist, and either press or tack to hold in position.

(4) Fold both sides of pleat A in to meet at the centre front. From the waistline down to the skirt hem, tack the pleats

into position to secure them temporarily. Now take the bodice section pattern piece and, with right side uppermost, position it behind the two free centre front bodice seams. Bring the two centre front seams in to meet at the centre of the upper bodice section, aligning the raw edges at the neckline. Tack the two seams into position. This seam is finished by hand, using an overcast stitch.

(5) Machine edge-stitch the centre front seams/pleats from the neckline down to the marks indicated on the pattern.

(6) Press along the entire length of the pleats and remove the tacking stitches. As before, the bottom edge of the hem pleats can be tacked into position to secure temporarily.

Joining the centre back panels

(7) Take the two back dress panels. With right sides together, join the centre back seam, leaving an 11.5cm (4½in) opening at the centre back neck. Press the seam open. If not utilizing the selvedge in the cut, neaten the seam allowance by trimming using pinking shears or trim and finish by hand using an overcast stitch.

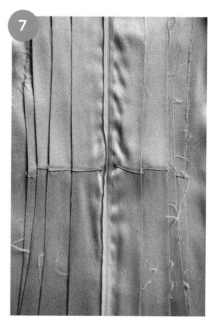

Centre back seam finish, from the inside.

Preparing the centre back panel pleats

(8) Now that the centre back seam has been joined, the pleats can be prepared. Working from the right side, fold the pleats marked E, F, G and H on the pattern in the direction indicated on the pattern, toward the centre back. Tack each pleat from the shoulders to the base of the skirt hem and press into position. Tack the pleats to secure, then machine edge-stitch the pleats from the shoulders down to the marks indicated on the pattern.

(9) Press along the entire length of the pleats and remove the tacking stitches.

As with the front dress panel, a tacking stitch can be run along the base of the hem to secure the pleats temporarily.

Trimming the front and back panel pleats

(10) To reduce bulk and to create a smoother silhouette, the pleats are trimmed and finished inside the dress. Start inside the front of the dress with pleat B; trim all the seam allowance layers from the neckline to the waistline to 1.2cm (½in) and finish by hand, securing all the layers with overcast stitching.

(11) For the remainder of this pleat and stopping 5cm (2in) above the base of the edge-stitching, cut away a section of the underside fabric, approximately 0.3cm (⅛in) in from the folded edge and approximately 0.7cm (¼in) in from the seam stitching.

(12) Machine top-stitch the edge where the fold was, to neaten.

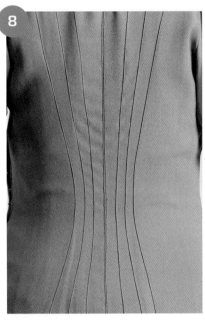

Edge-stitching on the centre back panel, from the right side.

Centre back pleats in position, from the right side.

Centre front pleat B, detail of trimmed finish.

Cut-away section of centre front, pleat B.

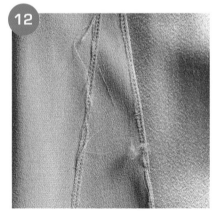

Centre front fold, top-stitching detail.

Cut-away section of centre front, pleat A.

Cut-away detail at dress front, pleat C.

Inside shaping dart on dress front, pleat C.

(13) Repeat the process (as described above for the lower portion of pleat B) for the centre front panel (pleat A).

(14) Next, trim pleat C by cutting away a section of the underside fabric, approximately 0.3cm (⅛in) in from the folded edge and approximately 0.7cm (¼in) in from the seam stitching. Machine top-stitch the edge where the fold was, to neaten.

(15) To ensure the pleated fabric inside the dress lies flat, a small dart must be created, approximately 4cm (1½in) below the waistline. The dart should measure 1.2cm (½in) (0.7cm (¼in) when stitched) at the fold edge and taper to a point 5cm (2in) across the pleat.

(16) For pleat D, repeat the processes described, apart from the finish to the free edge from the shoulder to the shaping dart. The raw edge on this section is trimmed completely flat and neatened by hand, using an overcast stitch.

(17) The section below the shaping dart is finished as before, using the

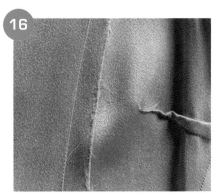

Upper section of dress front, pleat D.

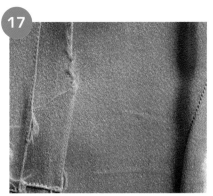

Stitched detail of pleat D, on the inside.

top-stitching method.

(18) Finally, secure all the free edges of the pleats together across the waistline by machining or hand-stitching through all the layers of fabric, from the outer edge of the centre front pleat,

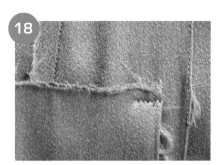

Centre front pleats secured inside.

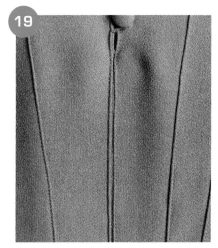

Centre back pleat E, neck detail, from the right side.

Back dress pleats, inside finish.

working horizontally across toward the centre of the dress panel. If working by hand, make the stitches approximately 1.2 cm (½in) deep.

(19) The back dress panel pleats E, F and G are treated in the same manner as front pleat C, so follow the instructions given previously. At the centre back neck opening on pleat E, simply fold across to the centre back seam and attach to the seam allowance.

(20) Pleat H is treated in the same manner as front pleat D, so follow the instructions given previously. The finished back dress panel pleats are left free and not attached together as in the front dress panel. Once the front and back dress panel pleats have all been trimmed and finished, it may be beneficial to run a line of tacking stitches across the pleats at each shoulder seam to secure the layers of fabric temporarily and ensure they lie flat and even for stitching.

Joining the front and back panels

(21) Take both prepared dress panels and, with right sides together, join the shoulder and side seams. Stitch the left side seam to the marks indicated on the pattern, leaving an opening of 17cm (6½in). Once all seams are stitched, remove the tacking stitches from the shoulder seams and press all the seams open. It may be necessary to clip into the side seams at the waist. In the original dress the shoulder seams are finished by hand using an overcast stitch.

(22) Finish the side seams by hand using an overcast stitch from armhole to waist; from the waist to the hem simply trim the allowance using pinking shears. If preferred, and for a

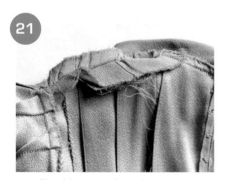

Shoulder seam, from the inside.

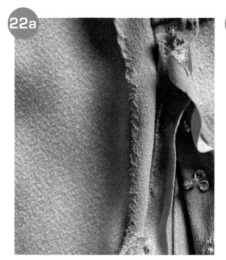

Dress side seam from the inside; overcast stitching.

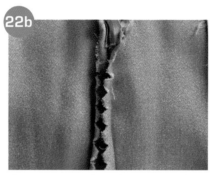

Dress side seam from the inside; pinked edges.

more polished look, the entire seam can be hand-sewn to finish.

Creating the side placket closure

(23) The placket closure at the left side seam is simply created by facing the opening. Begin by cutting two strips of the dress fabric measuring 20cm (8in) long x 2.5cm (1in) wide. Cut the strips with one long side utilizing the selvedge of the fabric, as this will avoid having to finish the edge of the placket facing once inserted. With right sides together, attach one strip onto each side of the opening, aligning the raw edges and stitching a 0.7cm (¼in) seam. The front facing side of the placket is finished by turning the facing to the inside of the dress and pressing flat, so the seamline is in alignment with the rest of the side seam.

Dress side opening placket, front edge.

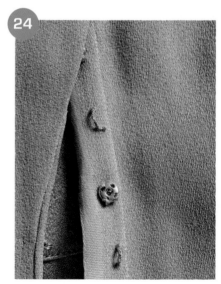

Dress side opening placket, back edge.

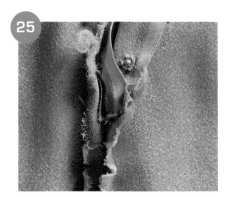

Placket ends on the inside.

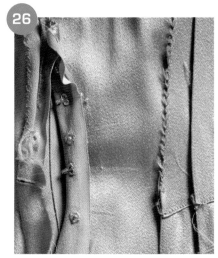

Placket front edge, press studs and hooks.

(24) The back facing side of the placket is pressed flat, toward the inside of the dress.

(25) Working on the inside of the dress, join the layers of each short end of the placket and attach them to the side seam with a few hand-stitches.

(26) To complete, attach alternate hooks and press studs along the front facing side of the placket, starting with a press stud approximately 1.2cm (½in) down from the top of the placket. Finish with a press stud approximately 1.2cm (½in) up from the bottom of the placket and position alternate hooks and press studs evenly between, using the remainder of the fastenings. The completed placket should contain a total of four press studs and three hooks.

(27) On the back facing side of the placket, attach corresponding studs and bars, ensuring the placket is aligned once closed and that it lies flat and even.

The original dress uses hand-worked bars but, if preferred, metal bars are just as suitable. A hand-worked bar is used where a couture finish is required or a fine fabric is being used to create the garment; the main point to remember is to create a fastening that is wide enough for the hook head to pass through easily, but tight enough to ensure the hook will remain in place whilst the garment is being worn. For the size of hook used in the dress, a 0.7cm (¼in) long bar should be sufficient. Line up the dress opening and mark with a pin on the back facing side of the placket where the centre point of the hook head will go through the bar.

(28) Using doubled sewing thread, anchor the end at the back of the fabric, then bring the needle through to the right side of the placket 0.3cm (⅛in) behind the pin and create a 0.7cm (¼in) back-stitch. Repeat to create a second stitch and ensure both are taut and even and that the hook head will pass through the loop. With the remaining thread, finish the bar by working a neat blanket stitch along the bar loop from one side to the other. This stitch is created by passing the needle under the bar loop, which will create a new loop above the bar. Bring the needle back through this new loop and pull downwards to create a knot. Repeat the process along the entire length of the bar and knot off securely once finished. It is essential that the thread is fixed well at both ends of the bar.

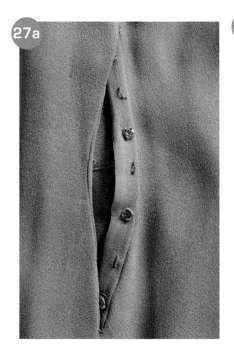

Placket back edge, press studs and bars.

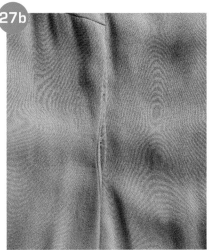

Side opening placket fastened.

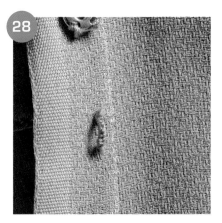

Hand-worked bar.

Preparing and inserting the sleeves
(29) Begin by stitching the darts at the sleeve head, as indicated on the pattern, and press them toward the centre of the sleeve head.

Sleeve head darts, from the inside.

Sleeve head darts, from the right side.

Underarm seam finish on the inside.

(30) Next, join the underarm seams to create the sleeves. Press the completed seams open and finish by hand using an overcast stitch.
(31) Prepare the sleeve hems by turning under the allowance indicated on the pattern and press to create a crisp fold; secure this hem by hand using a herringbone stitch.
(32) Take care to ensure the stitches on the right side are virtually invisible.

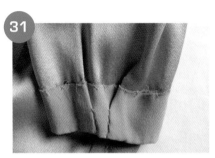
Sleeve hem, from the inside.

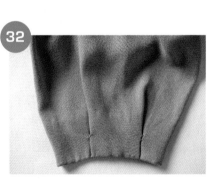
Sleeve hem pleats, from the right side.

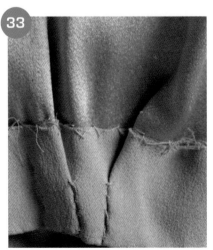
Sleeve hem pleats on the inside.

(33) The pleats at the sleeve hem can now be created. Working on the right side of the sleeve, fold the two pleats in the direction indicated on the pattern and secure by hand-sewing the folded edges onto the sleeve, using a slip-stitch. Stitch up from the hemline to a measurement of 2.5cm (1in). Repeat the process on the inside of the sleeve and, in addition, stitch across the base

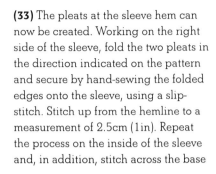
Sleeve inserted in armhole, from the inside.

Sleeve inserted in armhole, from the right side.

of the pleats to secure to the hem. Press to finish.

(34) The final stage is to insert the sleeves into the dress. With right sides together, insert the sleeve into the armhole, aligning the centre point of the sleeve head as indicated on the pattern with the shoulder seam and the underarm seam with the side seam. Ease the remaining seam allowance around the armhole, ensuring the sleeve darts lie flat at the shoulder. Stitch into position, then trim the seam allowance to 0.7cm (¼in) and finish by hand using an overcast stitch and securing all the layers together. Press the seam in toward the body of the dress.

Preparing and attaching the collar
(35) Begin by joining the ends of the collar. Fold the pattern piece in half lengthways, with right sides together. Stitch across the ends of the collar, trim the seam allowance to 0.3cm (⅛in) and turn right sides out. Press each finished end of the collar with the seamline positioned along the edge and very lightly press along the central fold to set the shape of the collar. The remaining raw edges of the neckline edge should be aligned and can be tacked together in preparation for attaching to the dress.

Collar fold detail, from the right side.

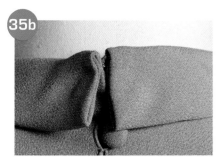
Collar ends detail, from the right side.

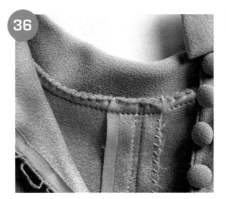
Collar seam finish, from the inside.

Completed collar, from the right side.

(36) Take the prepared collar and, with right sides together, position it along the neckline of the dress, starting at the centre front point and working round each side toward the centre back. Line up the ends of the collar with the finished centre back seam/opening.
(37) Stitch the collar into position and remove any tacking stitches. Trim the seam allowance to 0.7cm (¼in) and finish by hand using an overcast stitch, securing all the fabric layers. Press the seam up toward the folded edge of the collar.

Finishing the centre back neck opening
(38) The centre back neck opening is finished by the application of a button and loop fastening. Begin by covering six 1.2cm (½in) diameter buttons with the dress fabric and sew them onto the right-hand side of the opening, starting with the first button approximately 1.2cm (½in) down from the neckline (the measurement is taken from the centre of the button). Space the

Position of the buttons on the centre back neck opening.

Position of the loops on the centre back neck opening.

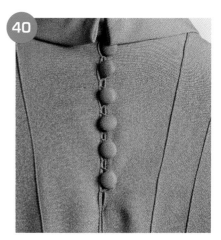
Button and loop closure fastened.

Hand-worked loops, detail.

remaining buttons evenly along the opening, finishing approximately 2.5cm (1in) above the base of the opening.

(39) On the left side of the opening, apply corresponding hand-worked loops.

(40) To make the loop to fasten the button, begin by marking out where the top and bottom of the loop should sit on the opening. The diameter of the button will dictate how wide the loop should be; to assist with this, place a pin just below the top and bottom edges of the button in position on the opening and this will give a sufficient guide to follow.

(41) Use doubled sewing thread approximately three times the length of the desired length of the loop and secure the end within the folds of fabric. Bring the needle up to the right side of the opening at the bottom pin marker. At the top pin marker, push the needle into the fabric and slide the needle back down the opening, bringing the needle back up at the lower pin. Pull the thread into a suitably sized loop that fits comfortably over the button and keeps the opening securely fastened without any gapping. Once the first loop has been created, repeat the process to make a second loop and finish by working a neat blanket stitch around the loop from one side to the other. This stitch is created by passing the needle under the button loop, which will create a new loop above. Bring the needle back through

this new loop and pull downwards to create a knot. Repeat the process around the entire length of the button loop and knot off securely once finished. It is essential that the thread is fixed well at both ends of the loop.

Finishing the skirt hem
(42) Begin by removing the tacking stitches from the base of the pleats at the centre front and centre back of the dress. Turn under the 2.5cm (1in) hem allowance and press to create a crisp, sharp edge. Secure the hem to the skirt

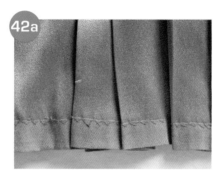

Skirt hem, from the inside.

Skirt hem, from the right side.

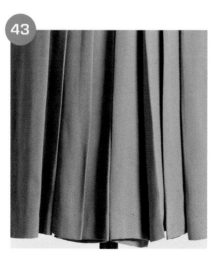

Skirt pleats, from the right side.

by hand, using a herringbone stitch, taking care to ensure the stitches on the right side are virtually invisible.
(43) Once complete, press to finish and make sure the skirt pleats are pressed back into place again.

Making Up the Cape
Preparing the centre back panel and pleat insert
(44) Begin by joining the centre back seam. With right sides together, join the centre back panels together from the neckline down to the mark indicated on the pattern. Press the

Upper centre back seam, from the inside.

Centre back pleat insert, from the inside.

seam open and do not trim any of the allowance as this will remain in the cape.

(45) Next, take the pleat insert pattern piece and, with right sides together, attach the insert at the two long edges to the unstitched sections of the centre back seam.

(46) Stitch the seams to 0.7cm (¼in) and clip into the top edge of the seam to release the centre back seam allowance. Press the pleat insert seams open.

(47) Now the centre back pleat can be created. Following the line indicated on the pattern, fold each side of the pleat in to meet at the centre line of the pleat

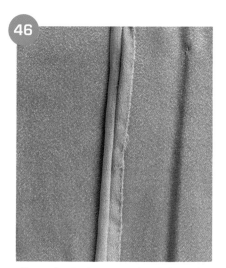

Centre back pleat seam detail, from the inside.

Centre back pleat inserted, from the right side.

insert. Press the pleat to create a crisp folded edge and tack across the base of the hemline to secure temporarily.

Joining the shoulder seams
(48) To join the cape at the shoulders, take the two front cape panels and the prepared back cape panel; with right sides together, join the shoulder seams. Once stitched, press the seams open. In the original dress the seam allowances have been left raw, but for a more complete and polished look, the raw edges can be finished by hand using an overcast stitch.

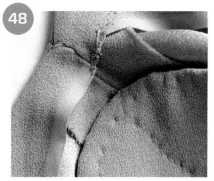

Shoulder seam detail, from the inside.

Creating and inserting the side panels and shoulder pads
(49) Start by creating the pleated detail on each side panel. Working on the right side and from the centre of the panel outwards, fold the pleats across toward the side seams as indicated on the pattern. Tack each pleat along its entire length and press to create a sharp fold. Next, measure down 10.5cm (4in) from the shoulder line and machine top-stitch a straight line across all the pleats. Repeat the process 2.5cm

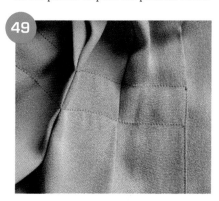

Side panel top stitching, detail.

Edge-stitching on the back panel side seam, detail.

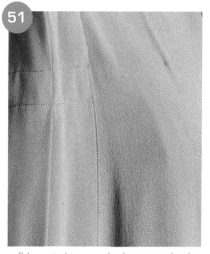

Edge-stitching on the front panel side seam, detail.

Side seam finish, on the inside.

(1in) below the first line of top-stitching to create two even, parallel lines across the pleats.

(50) Once this stage is complete, lay each side panel section flat and turn under the allowances at the side seams. Press to create a sharp fold. The prepared side panels are now ready to be attached to the front and back cape panels. With right sides uppermost, begin by laying each side panel at the side seam (back) onto the side seam of the back cape panel, positioning the folded edge 2.5cm (1in) in from the raw edge of the back panel side seam. Tack the joined seam to secure temporarily then machine edge-stitch from the mark indicated on the pattern, down to the base of the hemline. Do not attach the upper section of the side seam at this point.

(51) Repeat the process for the front cape panels so the entire cape is now joined.

(52) The inside seam allowance is simply neatened by trimming to 1.2cm (½in) using pinking shears. If preferred, the seam could be finished by hand, using an overcast stitch to secure all the layers. Press to finish.

(53) The next stage is to complete the shoulders. Start by turning under the 6.5cm (2½in) allowance, then press lightly to create a soft, folded edge which will become the shoulder head of the cape. Before attaching this

section, the shoulder pads must be prepared and inserted.

(54) Begin by covering the shoulder pads, which in the original dress have been simply covered using one pattern piece and tucking under a deep turning allowance. The allowance is folded and pleated around the pad and attached by hand using a tacking stitch.

If desired, the shoulder pads can be fully covered by cutting an extra pattern piece for each. With right sides together, stitch the two sections together around the curved edge, then trim and turn right sides out. Insert the shoulder pad and finish at the pad head by turning in the allowance and hand-sewing closed using a slip-stitch.

(55) Once the pad is covered, position it inside the cape, aligning the centre line of the pad with the shoulder seam of the cape. Line up the head of the

pad along the shoulder line of the cape and secure by hand-sewing through the shoulder seam and pad using a prick stitch.

(56) Tuck the shoulder line allowance over the pad and attach to the head of

Shoulder pad stitching, from the right side.

Cape side panel slip stitch detail of the upper section.

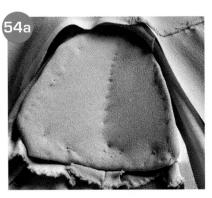

Shoulder pad attached, from the inside.

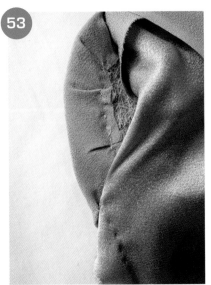

Folded fabric allowance on the shoulder pad.

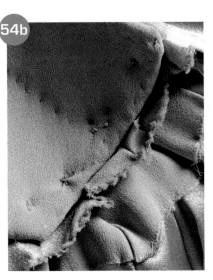

Detail of shoulder pad attached on the inside.

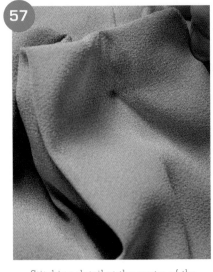

Stitching detail at the centre of the pleat.

the shoulder pad by hand using a few, small back-stitches.

(57) To complete the shoulder, the upper pleated section of the side panels must be attached. Following the line of the machine edge-stitching at the side seams, hand-sew the unattached folded edge onto the front and back panels, using a slip-stitch and stopping 2.5cm (1in) from the upper folded edge. Remove any tacking stitches.

(58) Now join the head of the pleated shoulder sections of each side panel to the end of the shoulder pad. Begin by locating the centre of the middle pleat and measure 2.5cm (1in) down from the upper folded edge. Attach the panel to the top edge of the shoulder pad, in line with the shoulder seam, using a few, small hand-stitches to secure through all the fabric layers.

(59) The upper edge of the side panel should naturally sit approximately 1.2cm (½in) above the shoulder. To attach the pleats on either side of the middle pleat, begin by locating the centre point 2.5cm (1in) down from the upper folded edge as before. At the back panel side, attach 1.2cm (½in) in) across the shoulder pad, from where the middle pleat is attached. At the front panel side, attach the pleat 2.5cm (1in) across the shoulder pad, from where the middle pleat is attached. Stitch both pleats, as before, on the top edge of the shoulder pad. The upper folded edge should sit approximately 1.2cm (½in) in) above the shoulder.

(60) The outer pleats are attached in the same manner but lie flat against the shoulder on both front and back panels. Finish by catching the top corner of each outer pleat to the cape using a few hand-stitches.

Finally, secure the raw edges of the panel allowance to the pleated section on the inside of the cape by hand, using an overcast stitch.

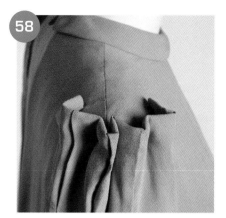

Pleats sitting above the shoulder.

Pleat attached at the front panel of the cape.

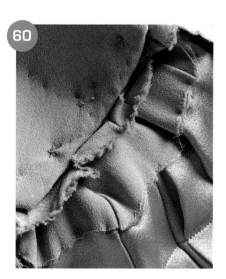

Inside sleeve head, showing the attaching stitches.

Creating the neckline and centre front facings

(61) Begin by taking the back neck facing pattern piece and, with right sides together, position it around the back neckline of the cape, aligning the raw edges. Stitch into position, stopping the stitching at either end of the shoulder seamline. Trim the seam allowance to 0.7cm (¼in), turn the facing to the inside of the cape and press so that the seamline sits just inside the back neckline. Secure the free edge of the facing to the centre back seam/shoulder seam allowances by hand using a herringbone stitch.

(62) The centre front facings can now be created. Using the line on the pattern for guidance, fold the centre front panels with right sides together. Stitch the facing allowance around the front neckline, aligning the raw edges and, as before, stitch just up to the shoulder seamlines. Trim the seam

Finish at the centre back neck facing, from the inside.

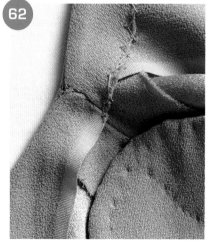

Stitching detail of the front facing shoulder attachment.

Hook at the centre front neck fastening.

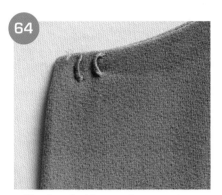

Hand-worked bars at the centre front neck fastening.

allowances to 0.7cm (¼in). Clip in at the corner where the centre front meets, to reduce bulk, and do the same around the curve of the neckline to aid turning out. Turn out the facings and fold back into the cape and press in the same manner as the back neck facing. Secure at the shoulder by folding under a 0.7cm (¼in) turning on the front facing and attach to the back facing by hand, using a slip-stitch. Press to finish.

(63) To complete the neckline closure, attach a hook to the right front panel at the corner point of the inside facing.

(64) Following the instructions described for the dress in Step 27 'Creating the side placket closure', create a hand-worked bar on the left front panel 1cm (⅜in) in from the centre front edge and positioned vertically on the fabric. The original cape has an extra bar attached for adjustability.

Finishing the cape hem

(65) Begin by removing the tacking stitches holding the back panel pleat in position. Next, turn under a 5cm (2in) hem, as indicated on the pattern, along the entire hemline, including the centre front facings. Press to create a sharp fold and secure temporarily using a tacking stitch. Now fold the centre front facings back into the cape, press to reinstate the fold and secure to the hem by hand using a slip-stitch.

(66) Complete the hem by securing the remainder to the cape by hand, using a herringbone stitch, ensuring the stitches are virtually invisible on the right side.

(67) Press to finish, including the centre back pleat.

Front facing at the cape hem, from the inside.

Cape hem finish, from the inside.

Cape hem finish, from the right side.

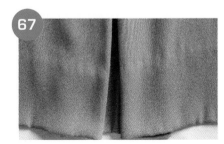

Completed centre back pleat hem, from the right side.

Detail of buttons on green
tailored dress.

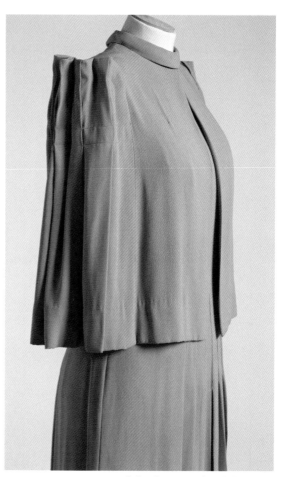

Side of green tailored dress and
matching cape.

Shoulder detail of green
tailored dress and
matching cape.

TAILORED DAY DRESS & MATCHING CAPE
SCALE 1:5 FOR ALL PATTERN PIECES ON THIS PAGE

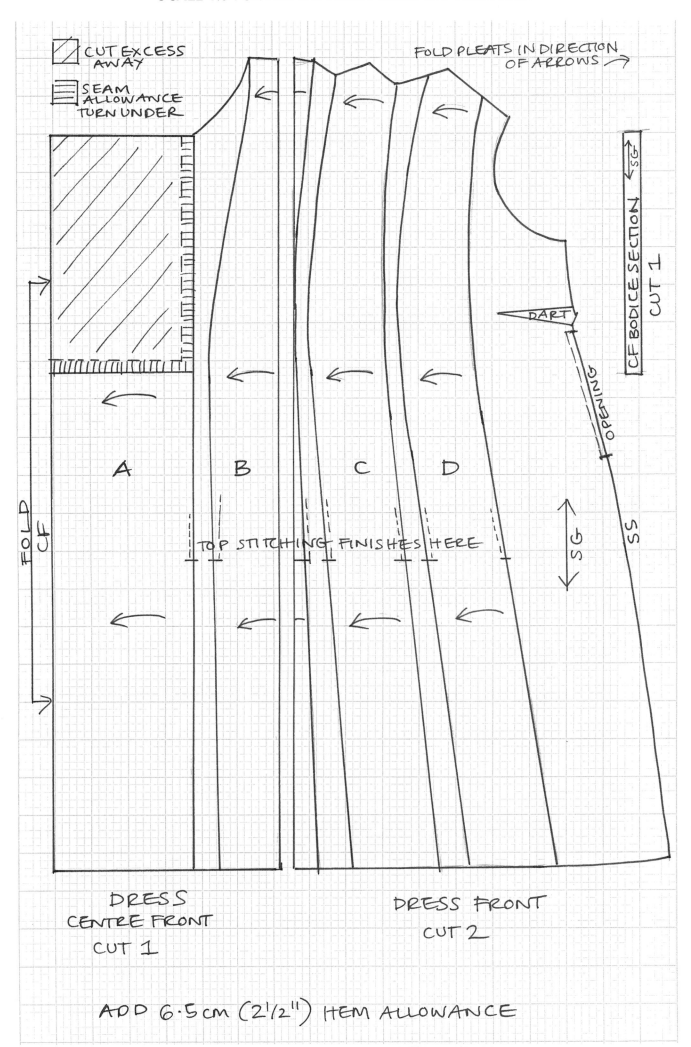

CUT EXCESS AWAY

SEAM ALLOWANCE TURN UNDER

FOLD PLEATS IN DIRECTION OF ARROWS →

CF BODICE SECTION
CUT 1
SG

DART

OPENING

FOLD
CF

A   B   C   D

TOP STITCHING FINISHES HERE

SG

SS

DRESS
CENTRE FRONT
CUT 1

DRESS FRONT
CUT 2

ADD 6·5 cm (2½") HEM ALLOWANCE

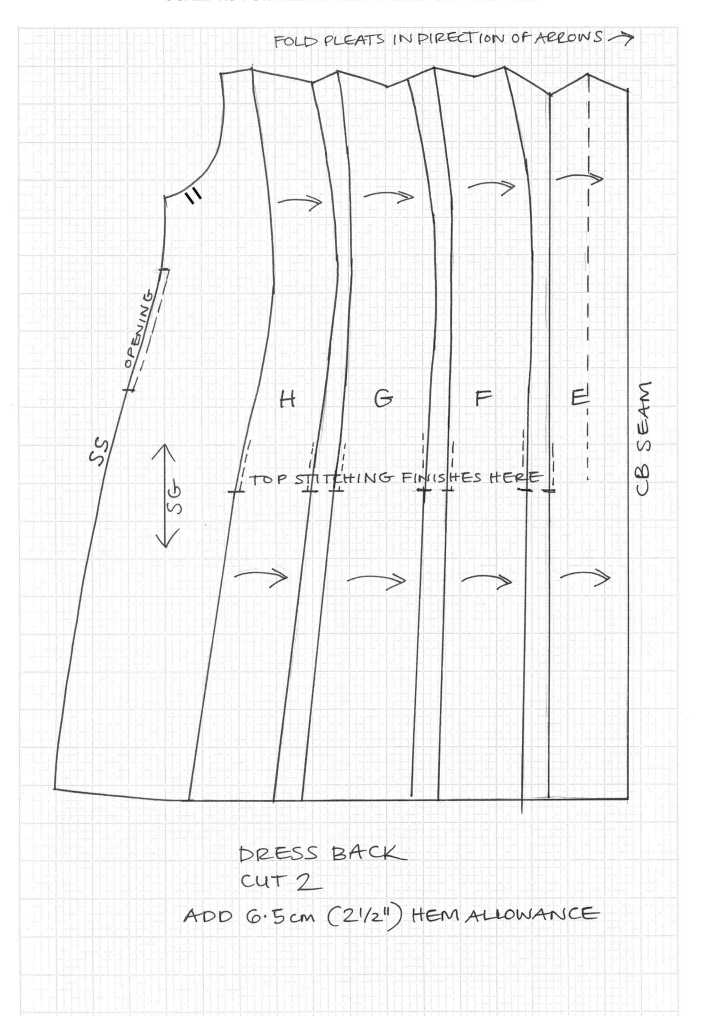

FOLD PLEATS IN DIRECTION OF ARROWS →

OPENING

SS

SG

H   G   F   E

TOP STITCHING FINISHES HERE

CB SEAM

DRESS BACK
CUT 2
ADD 6·5cm (2½") HEM ALLOWANCE

TAILORED DAY DRESS & MATCHING CAPE
SCALE 1:5 FOR ALL PATTERN PIECES ON THIS PAGE

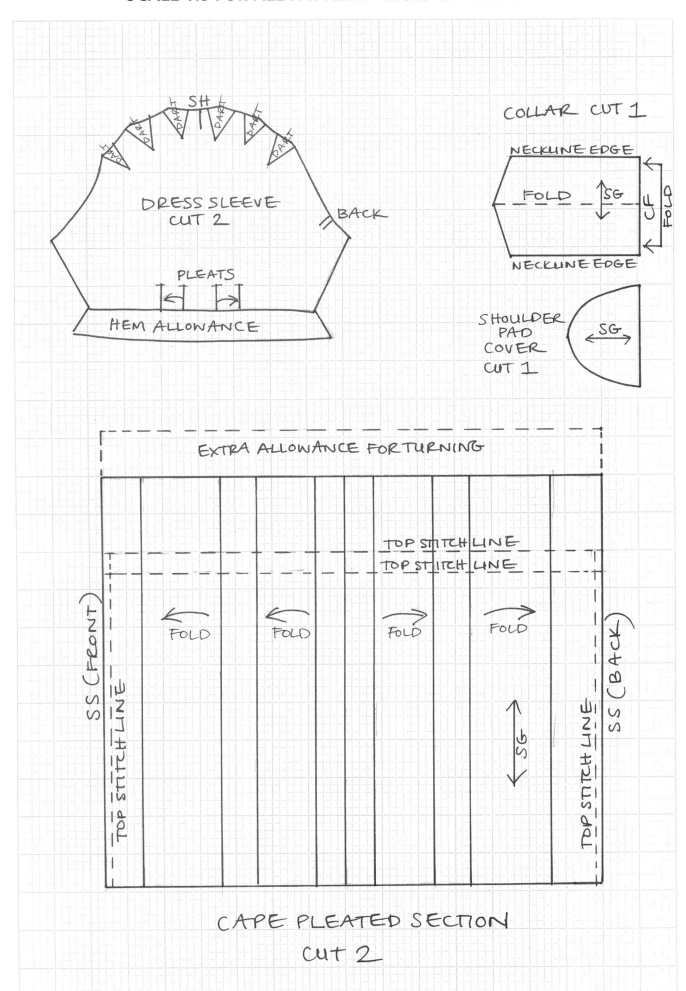

SH

DART DART DART DART DART

DRESS SLEEVE
CUT 2

BACK

PLEATS

HEM ALLOWANCE

COLLAR CUT 1

NECKLINE EDGE

FOLD SG CF FOLD

NECKLINE EDGE

SHOULDER
PAD
COVER
CUT 1

SG

EXTRA ALLOWANCE FOR TURNING

TOP STITCH LINE
TOP STITCH LINE

SS (FRONT)

TOP STITCH LINE

FOLD FOLD FOLD FOLD

SG

SS (BACK)

TOP STITCH LINE

CAPE PLEATED SECTION

CUT 2

TAILORED DAY DRESS & MATCHING CAPE
SCALE 1:5 FOR ALL PATTERN PIECES ON THIS PAGE

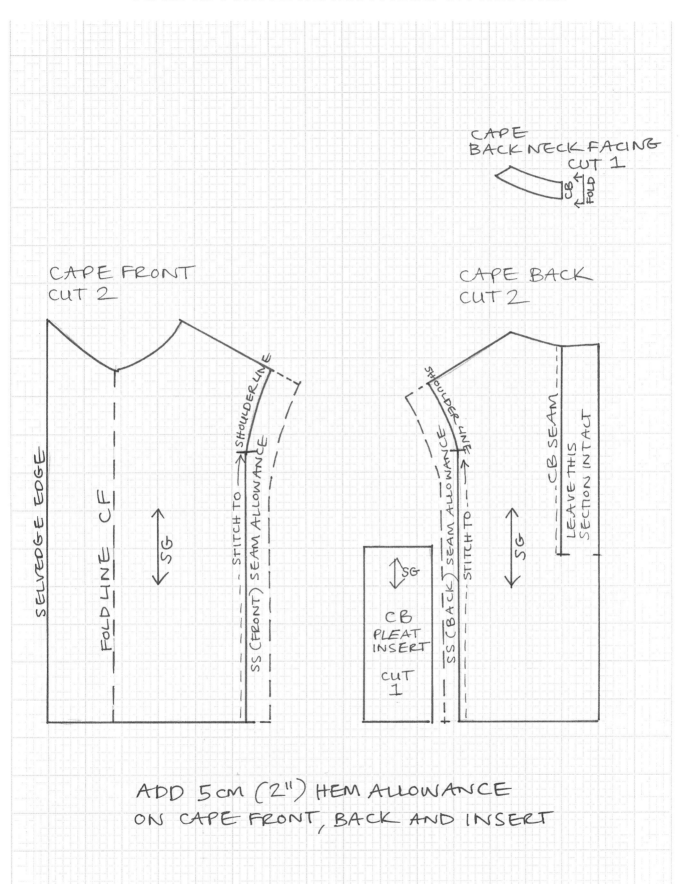

CAPE
BACK NECK FACING
CUT 1

CB FOLD

CAPE FRONT
CUT 2

CAPE BACK
CUT 2

SELVEDGE EDGE

FOLD LINE CF

SG

SHOULDER LINE

STITCH TO →

SS (FRONT) SEAM ALLOWANCE

SHOULDER LINE

← STITCH TO

SS (BACK) SEAM ALLOWANCE

SG

CB SEAM

LEAVE THIS SECTION INTACT

SG

CB
PLEAT
INSERT

CUT
1

ADD 5 cm (2") HEM ALLOWANCE
ON CAPE FRONT, BACK AND INSERT

Evening Dress and Matching Cape

10

This stunning evening dress and matching shoulder cape exude glamour, with their sleek styling and the subtle sparkle of the perfectly placed beaded decoration on the front bodice. The dress and cape are made from a mid-weight satin, which has been cut on the bias grain to allow for drape and body-skimming shaping. The dress is sleeveless with a plunging V-shaped front and back neckline. The neckline and armholes are bound using the dress fabric and the inside shoulder seams have ribbon brassiere retainers attached.

The lower part of the bodice is V-shaped at the front and the back, echoing the neckline and elongating the silhouette. The panels are cut using the reverse and right sides of the fabric to add contrast and accentuate the sharp, geometric cut of the dress. The beaded decoration also reflects the shaping of the dress, with its straight, angled lines; a combination of silver-lined bugle and seed beads, along with diamanté stones, has been used to great effect.

A fluid, circular-shaped skirt falls from the hip to the floor, adding fullness and movement to the dress. The skirt hem is finished using a picot edge which keeps the skirt light. The dress is unlined and has no fastenings.

The short, circular-shaped shoulder-length cape is made from the satin fabric used in the dress and ties at the neck, its simple styling complementing and slightly softening the angular lines of the dress. The hem is finished with the same picot edge as the skirt.

Back of black satin evening dress with matching cape.

Left: Black satin evening dress with matching cape.

Instructions for Making Up the Dress and Cape

To start

Begin by cutting out all the pattern pieces for the dress, adding seam and hem allowances, and set them aside.

Making Up the Dress

Applying the decoration to the bodice

(1) The original dress has a beaded decoration applied to the centre front bodice in a striking geometric design and the pattern uses a combination of silver-lined glass bugle and seed beads, alongside flat-back rhinestones.
(2) From the inside of the dress, it can be seen that this was professionally

Beaded decoration, from the right side.

MEASUREMENTS

Bust: 81.5cm (32in)

Waist: 71/74cm (28/29in)

Hips: 96.5cm (38in)

Approximate dress size: UK 10/12, US 6/8, EU 38/40

FABRIC SUGGESTIONS AND NOTIONS

Fabrics such as satins and silk satins with a soft sheen work perfectly for this style of dress. For a lighter feel, jersey knits would also be suitable, but extra care would be required when stitching and applying the decoration due to the extra stretch within the fabric. The fabric must drape well and be of a suitable weight to lie on the body without clinging. For a really personalized and individual look, contrasts of fabric and beading colours could be used to striking effect.

Matching sewing thread

Bugle/seed beads and rhinestones/crystals for bodice decoration

9cm (3½in) of 0.7/1cm (¼/⅜in) wide ribbon (matching the dress fabric colour)

2 x 0.7cm (¼in) press studs

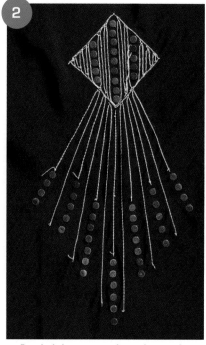

Beaded decoration, from the inside.

11 STEPS TO CREATE A 1930s EVENING DRESS AND MATCHING CAPE

1. Cut out all the pattern pieces

Dress:

2. Apply the decoration to the bodice

3. Join the panels to the front bodice

4. Join the panels to the back bodice

5. Join the front and back bodice sections

6. Finish the neckline and armholes

7. Join the skirt panels

8. Attach the skirt to the bodice

9. Finish the skirt hem

Cape:

10. Finish the cape edges

11. Prepare and attach the neck tie

applied using the tambour technique, whereby the decoration is worked from the reverse side of the fabric, using a tambour hook, and the flat-back rhinestones are applied using a metal clip backing. The application of the decoration using this technique should only be attempted by those experienced in using it, as the tambour hook is tricky to master for the beginner.

The decoration on the dress consists of a series of straight lines and so should be quite easy to apply from the right side of the fabric. There are numerous methods for transferring an embroidery or beading pattern to fabric and there is much literature available and online tutorials to this end. For this dress it is advisable to use the least invasive method that avoids the use of transfers that require wet cleaning to remove them: this has the potential to cause watermarks, discolouration and even running of dyes.

The simplest method would be to tack the basic outline shape into position on the right side of the fabric and follow the lines of beading just alongside the tacking stitches, which can then be easily removed. An alternative would be to trace the pattern onto light tracing paper, which is then tacked onto the right side of the fabric and used as a guide, upon which the beads are stitched, through the paper and onto the fabric. Once the decoration is applied, the tracing paper is carefully torn away from the fabric, leaving the beaded pattern in position. For this method to be successful, the beads must be securely applied.

Finally, and if a finer fabric is being used and therefore more substance required, the pattern can be traced onto a piece of organza, matching the dress colour and to the dimensions of the pattern. This is then positioned on the wrong side of the fabric to be decorated and secured in place using a running or tacking stitch, following the lines of the design. Use a sewing thread that matches the fabric colour so that when the beads are applied on the right side, the lines of the pattern will be visible enough to follow, but not seen once the decoration is complete.

To apply the beads, use a fine-gauge or beading needle and apply to the fabric using a back-stitch. The seed beads can be applied two or three at a time for speed and using a lightly waxed or doubled thread will ensure the lines of beading lie straight and even. With any application of a beaded or embroidered decoration, the best results are achieved when the base fabric is held taut, across a frame or embroidery hoop. With this dress, extra care should be taken to position the bodice pattern piece correctly in the frame or hoop, so that the tension is across the straight grain. Cut the pattern piece within a rectangular or larger section of fabric for ease of manoeuvrability and to avoid overstretching.

Joining the panels to the front bodice

The design of the V-shaped dress panels uses both right and wrong sides of the fabric to create contrast; ensure

Front bodice V-shaped panels, from the right side.

Front bodice V-shaped panels, from the inside.

Seam finish detail on the inside.

the directions on the pattern are followed closely when cutting these pieces.

(3) To make up, begin by taking panels A and B; place the wrong side of A's

Front bodice V-shaped panels joined, from the right side.

Back bodice V-shaped panels joined, from the right side.

lower edge to the right side of B's upper edge and join the panel seam by machine stitching, ensuring the points are sharp.

(4) It will be necessary to clip into the seam allowance to ease the fabric into the point.

(5) Once joined, press the seam open and finish the raw edges by turning under 0.3cm (⅛in) and machine edge-stitching the seam allowance to neaten.

(6) Next, join the newly formed V-shaped panel to the front bodice panel by attaching the wrong side of A's upper edge to the right side lower edge of the bodice panel. Stitch together and finish the seam allowance on the inside, using the same method as before.

Joining the panels to the back bodice

(7) The back V-shaped panels marked C and D on the pattern are joined using exactly the same method as the front bodice panels and the inside seam finishing is carried out in the same manner as before. As with the front bodice panels, ensure the points are sharp and clip into the seam allowance as necessary to ease with manoeuvring the fabric.

Joining the front and back bodice sections

(8) The front and back bodice sections are joined using French seams to create the side and shoulder seams. Start creating this twice-stitched seam by placing the wrong sides of the fabric together and then stitching the seam in the usual manner, after which the seam is pressed open. Next, trim the raw edges of the seam allowance to approximately 1cm (⅜in), ready to complete the second stage. This will ensure that no fibres protrude from the finished French seam on the right side of the fabric.

The second stage in creating the seam is to fold the fabric back on itself, so the right sides are now facing one another and the raw edges of the first seam are completely enclosed. Stitch a 0.7cm (¼in) wide seam and finish by pressing the seam toward the back of

Dress side seam, from the inside.

Dress side seam, from the right side.

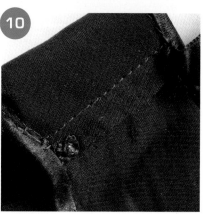

Shoulder seam detail, from the inside.

the garment.

(9) Take extra care and time to align the seamlines of the V panels accurately at the side seams to create a sharp, angled line and give a professional finish.

(10) Join the shoulder seams in the same manner and press in the direction of the back neckline to finish.

Finishing the neckline and armholes

(11) The neckline and armholes are simply and elegantly finished using a narrow self-binding made from the dress fabric. Begin by cutting three strips of the dress fabric on the bias grain, all measuring approximately 2.5cm wide and about 96.5cm (38in) long for the neckline and 53.5cm (21in) long for each armhole. It may be necessary to join strips of the binding to make a sufficient length; when doing so, always join the sections diagonally across the straight grain. Before attaching a section of joined binding, if possible try to position the join where it will not be noticeable, especially on an area such as the front bodice neckline where a smooth, continuous line is desirable.

Attach the binding to the neckline and armholes using the following method. Start by machine-stitching a straight stay-stitch around the raw edges at the neckline and armholes to reduce the likelihood of the fabric stretching whilst the binding is applied. Make the stitch line 0.3cm (⅛in) in from the raw edge. Next, with right sides of the fabric together, position the binding strip along the area of the garment to be bound, aligning the raw edges. Gently stretch the binding strip as it is being positioned around any curved areas, to ensure the line is neat and tight. At the V points on the neckline, it will be necessary to create a small fold.

Stitch the binding strips into position, just outside the tacking/stay-stitch line. Once each strip is stitched, carefully and gently press the binding up toward the raw edge using the tip of the iron. This will help create a smooth seam edge. The next stages are worked from the inside of the dress.

(12) Now take the remaining raw edge of the binding and fold it in half so that the raw edge sits behind the seam allowance and touches the seam. Next, fold in half again, so the top fold touches the seam stitches; secure this edge along the stitching line by hand, using a slip-stitch. Carefully press the finished binding to create a neat, sharp edge.

(13) Once the binding has been

Bodice binding finish, from the right side.

Bodice binding finish, from the inside.

completed, the next stage is to create and attach the brassiere retainers at the shoulders. Working on the inside of the dress, take two small sections of ribbon approximately 4.5cm (1¾in) long, make a double turn of 0.3cm (⅛in) at one end of each and secure around the edges by hand using a slip-stitch. Once stitched, attach one part of a press stud to each ribbon piece. At the opposite end of each ribbon piece, turn under 0.7cm (¼in) and, working on the inside of the shoulder seams, hand-sew the turned end of the ribbon pieces 0.3cm

Brassiere retainer at the shoulder seam, unfastened.

Brassiere retainer at the shoulder seam, fastened.

(⅛in) in from the outer edge of each armhole binding.

(14) To finish, attach the other part of the press stud on the opposite side of the shoulder seam on each side, at the neckline edge. Position the fastening so that, when closed, the brassiere retainer lies flat.

Joining the skirt panels

(15) With right sides together, join the skirt panels using a straight seam and press open to finish. In the original dress the selvedge edges have been utilized in the cut and therefore no finishing was required. If not using this method, the seam allowances can be finished to preference by being left raw or trimmed using pinking shears or, for a finer finish, the allowance can be hand-sewn using an overcast stitch.

Skirt seam, from the inside.

Attaching the skirt to the bodice

(16) Find the centre front and centre back points on the skirt waist and mark with a pin or small tacking stitch. With right sides together, attach the skirt to the bodice, aligning the side seams and centre points with the pointed ends of the front and back bodice sections. Clip into the points as necessary to aid manipulation of the seam allowance, then stitch the bodice and skirt together. Press the seam

Pointed joins, detail, from the inside.

Seam finish, skirt and bodice join, detail, from the inside.

Skirt and bodice joined, from the inside.

allowance up in the direction of the bodice.

(17) The seam allowance is finished by machining a second row of stitching approximately 0.3cm (⅛in) above the seamline just created; trim away the excess to neaten.

Finishing the skirt hem

(18) The skirt hem of the dress is neatened with a decorative picot edge, a popular finish in garments of this era and often found in high-end couture pieces. The beauty of this method of stitching and how it suits this style of dress is the fact that it creates a fine, lightweight hem that enhances the fluidity of shaping and cut. A picot edge is often used on circular-shaped hemlines and with fine fabrics due to its ability to create extra fullness and swing on the fabric edge.

A true picot edge is created using a specialist machine and pressure foot, but a similar effect can be achieved using a regular sewing machine. The skirt hem can be created using a roll hemming pressure foot in conjunction with a zig-zag stitch. The fabric is run through the roll hemming foot in the usual manner, but using a zig-zag stitch rather than a straight stitch in order to create the decorative finish.

It is always a good idea to test the stitching on an offcut of the dress fabric first, before attempting to tackle the dress itself. Try different stitch lengths and widths to gauge how the fabric will react. The original dress uses a very narrow, close stitch in order to give a fine finish to the skirt hem.

Alternatively, the raw edges of the hem can be machined using a narrow, close zig-zag stitch and finished by trimming away any excess fabric fibres along the hem edge. Press the hem to finish.

Hem finish detail, from the inside.

Hem finish detail, from the right side.

Making Up the Cape
Finishing the cape edges

(19) The cape's centre front edges and hemline are neatened in the same manner as the skirt, with a decorative picot finish, as described above under the heading 'Finishing the skirt hem'. Take the main cape pattern piece and create a picot-style hem down each centre front edge and around the hemline. Leave the neckline raw and press to finish.

Preparing and attaching the neck tie

(20) To create the cape's neck tie, start by taking the cut piece and, with right sides together, fold in half lengthways to make what will be the top edge, as indicated on the pattern. Stitch in from each pointed end to the marks indicated on the pattern and trim the seam allowances to 0.7cm (¼in). Trim across the pointed ends and corners to reduce bulk, then turn right side out. Press the neck tie so the seamline lies

Cape completed.

Cape centre front edge and hem finish.

Cape neck tie, pointed end.

Neck tie, neckline end, from the right side.

along the edge and the pointed ends are sharp and neat.

(21) The next stage is to join the neck tie to the cape. Working on the wrong side of the cape, position the right side of one free edge of the neck tie along the neckline, aligning the raw edges. The hemmed edges at the centre front of the cape should meet at the stitched end of the necktie.

(22) Stitch the neckline seam and trim the seam allowance to 0.7cm (¼in) and press up into the neck tie.

(23) Bring the remaining free edge over to the right side to cover the seam stitches. Turn under a hem of 0.3cm (⅛in) and press lightly to create a folded edge. Position this edge approximately 0.3cm (⅛in) below the seamline and tack into position temporarily. Working from the right side of the cape, machine top-stitch along the neckline, securing the folded hem. Press to finish.

Neck tie joined to the neckline, from the inside.

Neckline top-stitching, from the right side.

Black satin evening dress with matching cape.

Beading on black satin evening dress.

EVENING DRESS AND CAPE
SCALE 1:5 FOR ALL PATTERN PIECES ON THIS PAGE

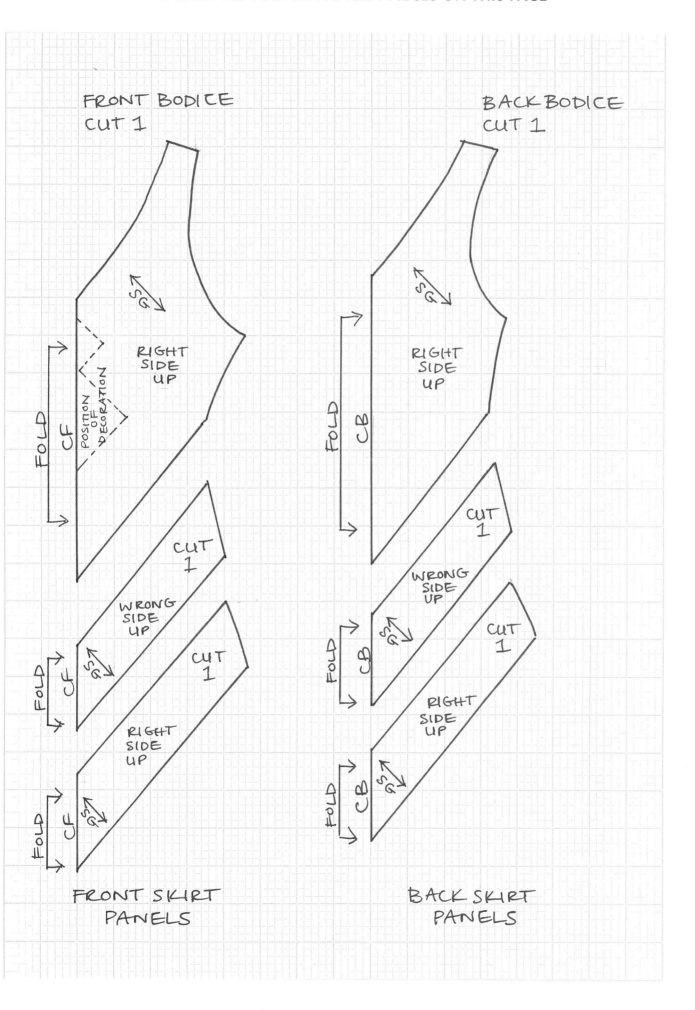

FRONT BODICE
CUT 1

BACK BODICE
CUT 1

SG

RIGHT SIDE UP

FOLD

CF

POSITION OF DECORATION

SG

RIGHT SIDE UP

FOLD

CB

CUT 1

CUT 1

WRONG SIDE UP

WRONG SIDE UP

FOLD

CF

SG

SG

CB

FOLD

CUT 1

CUT 1

RIGHT SIDE UP

RIGHT SIDE UP

FOLD

CF

SG

FOLD

CB

SG

FRONT SKIRT PANELS

BACK SKIRT PANELS

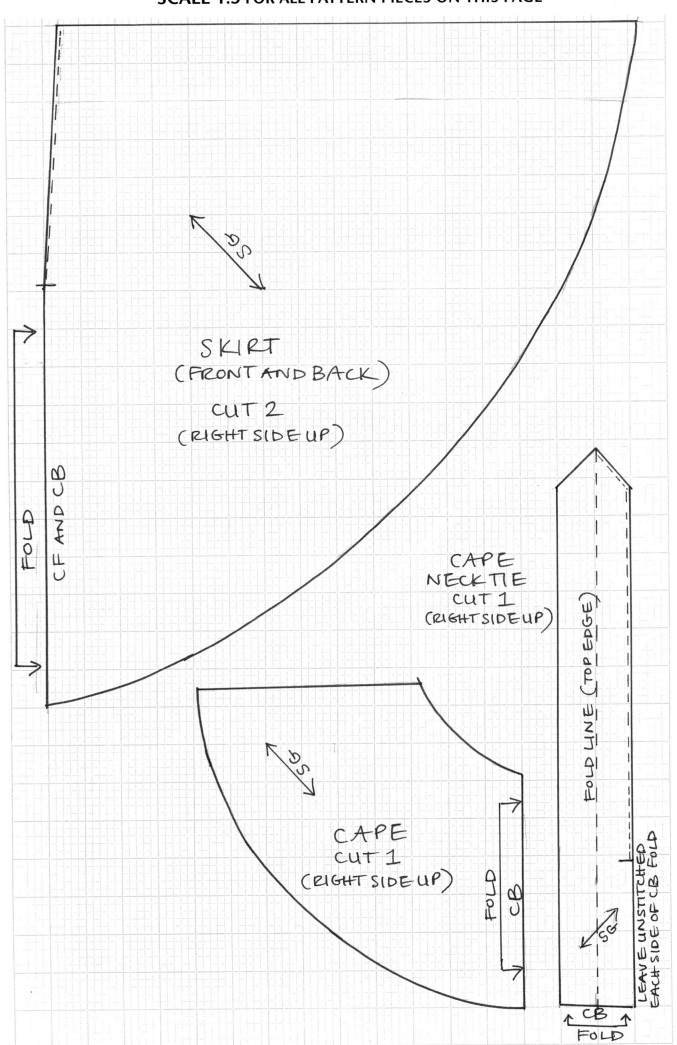

SG

SKIRT
(FRONT AND BACK)

CUT 2
(RIGHT SIDE UP)

FOLD

CF AND CB

CAPE
NECKTIE
CUT 1
(RIGHT SIDE UP)

SG

CAPE
CUT 1
(RIGHT SIDE UP)

FOLD

CB

FOLD LINE (TOP EDGE)

LEAVE UNSTITCHED
EACH SIDE OF CB FOLD

SG

CB

FOLD

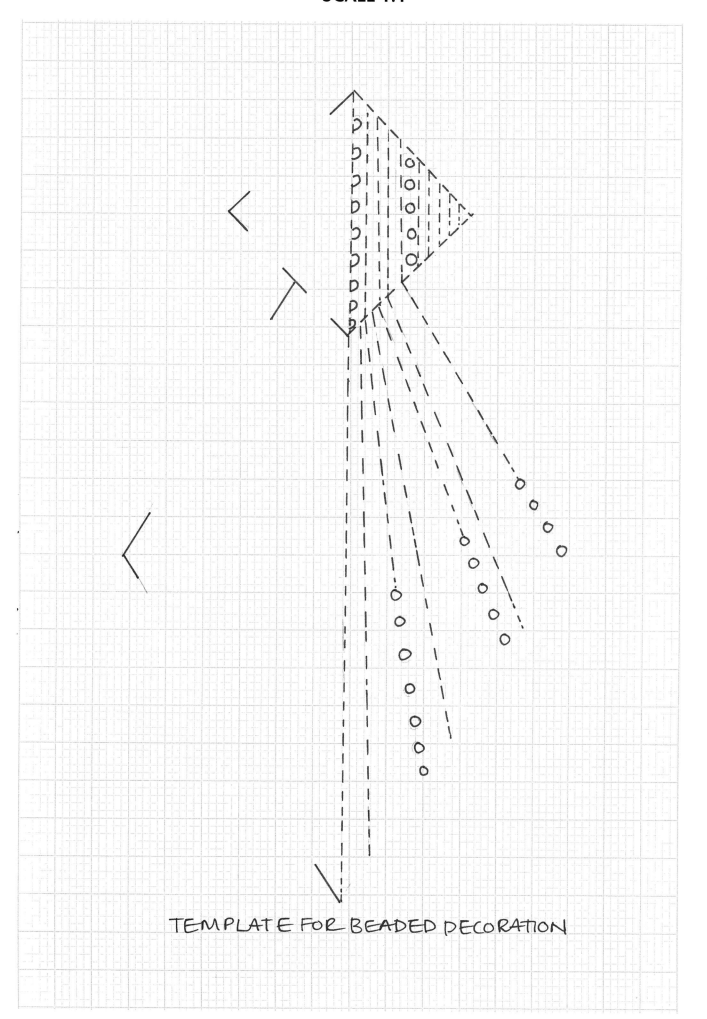

TEMPLATE FOR BEADED DECORATION

Velvet Evening Dress

This striking, full-length evening dress has classic styling with its bias cut and understated glamour. The fabric is a sumptuous electric blue devoré (burnout) silk velvet with stylized leaf design. The bodice is sleeveless with a deep V neckline at the centre front, which is embellished with a rich, ruched velvet trim in the same electric blue. The trim lies across the front left side of the bodice from the shoulder to just below the neckline and on the right side from the shoulder across the body and finishing at the left hip. The detail at the left hip is further enhanced with the addition of four bow tails in the dress fabric, which drape onto the skirt.

The back bodice has an asymmetrical centre back seam, gathered on the left side to create a softly draped effect, and the neckline and armholes are simply faced using cotton bias binding. The unusual angled cut of the skirt panels and bodice add an element of structure to this essentially soft and loose-fitting dress. The skirt hem is finished using a decorative picot edge.

The dress is unlined, with no fastenings, and would originally been worn with a lightweight silk slip underneath. The inside seam allowances of the dress are finished using various methods: either left raw, trimmed using pinking shears, or utilizing the selvedge of the fabric. French seams are used in the bodice.

Side view of blue devoré velvet evening dress.

Left: Blue devoré velvet evening dress.

Instructions for Making Up the Dress

To start

Begin by cutting out all the pattern pieces for the dress, adding seam and hem allowances, and set them aside. It is important to note that velvets have a definite direction of pile (nap) and each pattern piece must be placed with the pile running in the same direction. To do this, use tailor's chalk to draw a small arrow on the wrong side of each piece. This will ensure there is no difference in shade/tone when the garment is sewn.

Joining the back bodice panels

(1) Begin by running two parallel rows of gathering stitches along the centre

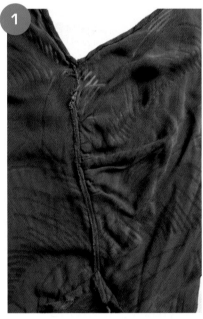

Gathered centre back panel, from the inside.

MEASUREMENTS

Bust: 89/91.5cm (35/36in)

Waist: 81.5/84cm (32/33in)

Hips: 94/96.5cm (37/38in)

Approximate dress size: UK 12/14, US 8/10, EU 40/42

FABRIC SUGGESTIONS AND NOTIONS

The obvious choice for this dress is velvet and the options available are endless, for colour, pattern and finish. Devoré velvet will give the dress not only colour and bold pattern but an allure created by the contrast between the solid and semi-sheer elements of the fabric. If a more solid finish is desired, crushed pile velvet fabrics give sufficient coverage but fantastic texture and sheen. Soft, satin fabrics with plenty of drape are an alternative to velvet if preferred and will show off the geometric cut to good effect. A beaded or diamanté trim would look spectacular against a satin fabric.

Matching sewing thread

78cm (30½in) length of 4cm (1½in) wide ruched velvet trim

91.5cm (36in) length of 0.7cm (¼in) wide bias binding to match the dress colour

back seam on the left back bodice pattern piece, as indicated on the pattern. Start the stitches just inside where the seamline will be and run the second row 0.7cm (¼in) behind the first, so that they both sit within the seam allowance. The stitches can be by hand or machine. Pull the gathers up to match the measurement of the centre back seam on the right back bodice pattern piece and secure by tying off the threads.

Next, turn under the seam allowance on the centre back seam of the right bodice panel; with right sides uppermost, position the folded edge onto the gathered seam of the left bodice panel so that it just covers the gathering stitches. Align the top and bottom points of the centre back seam and tack into position ready for stitching. Make sure the tacking

11 STEPS TO CREATE A 1930s VELVET EVENING DRESS

1. Cut out all the pattern pieces

2. Join the back bodice panels

3. Join the bodice side and shoulder seams

4. Finish the neckline and armholes

5. Join the centre front bodice seam

6. Join the front and back skirt panels

7. Join the front and back skirt sections

8. Join the bodice and skirt

9. Finish the skirt hem

10. Apply the front bodice neckline trim

11. Create and attach the bow tails

stitches are not too tight, as velvet fabrics can mark easily.

(2) Working on the right side of the bodice, machine top-stitch the centre back seam, then remove the tacking stitches. The seam allowance is finished on the inside by simply

Centre back seam top-stitching, from the right side.

PRESSING VELVET FABRICS

Velvets are easily crushed and should only be pressed by steaming from the wrong side, holding the iron just above the fabric and not placing it directly onto the surface. For the best results a velvet needle board or mat should be used whereby the velvet is laid right side down onto the board and the small needles separate the fibres of the pile, preventing it from being flattened. If a needle board is not available then using another piece of velvet pile up is an alternative; the velvets should be laid right sides together, pile on pile, and then steamed.

Take care when steaming that your hands are protected and use another piece of velvet as a pressing cloth if necessary. It is always advisable to test on an offcut of the fabric being used before pressing the garment.

trimming back to just above the second row of gathering stitches.

Joining the bodice side and shoulder seams
(3) Begin by joining the bodice side seams using a French seam. Start by placing the wrong sides of the fabric together; stitch the seam in the usual manner and then press the seam open. Next, trim both raw edges of the seam allowance to approximately 1cm (⅜in) in width, ready to complete the second stage. This will ensure that no fibres protrude from the finished French seam, on the right side of the fabric.

The second stage in creating the seam is to fold the fabric back on itself, so the right sides are now facing one another and the raw edges of the first seam are completely enclosed. Stitch a 0.7cm (¼in) wide seam.
(4) Once the side seams are completed, the shoulder seams can be joined.

Bodice side French seam, from the inside.

Shoulder seam gathering stitches, from the inside.

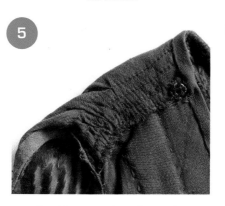

Shoulder seam, from the inside.

Begin by sewing two rows of running stitches, by hand, across the back bodice shoulder seams. In this instance, the stitches will be visible on the garment. Start the first row 0.3cm (⅛in) below where the seamline will be; the second row of stitching is positioned 0.3cm (⅛in) below the first. As these stitches will form part of the finish on the dress, make sure they are small, neat and straight.

Neckline binding at the centre front, from the inside.

Neckline binding at the centre back, from the inside.

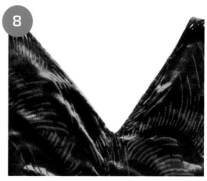

Neckline binding detail, from the right side.

119

9a

Armhole binding detail, on the inside.

9b

Armhole binding detail, from the right side.

Finishing the neckline and armholes

(6) The neckline and armholes are simply finished with the application of a narrow, cotton bias binding. With right sides together and starting at one of the shoulder seams, apply the bias binding around the neckline, aligning the raw edges and taking care to fold at the points to ensure it will lie flat once turned in. At each end, fold over a small turning, then stitch the binding into position.

(7) Fold the binding over to the inside of the dress and secure to the fabric by hand, using a slip-stitch.

(8) At the centre front and back points, the binding is pleated and attached to itself by hand, using a slip-stitch. From the right side the binding should not be visible.

(9) Repeat the process for the armholes, but in this instance the binding should be stretched gently around the curved areas to ensure it lies flat once folded inside the dress.

Joining the centre front bodice seam

(10) The centre front bodice seam can now be joined in preparation for attaching to the skirt. Working on the right side, lay the left front bodice panel over the right, aligning the centre front seamlines. Secure the join

temporarily by tacking along the seamline. The application of the trim will eventually hold the seam together and the extra seam allowance added to the left-hand panel will give more substance to the seam.

Joining the front and back skirt panels

(11) Depending on the width of fabric used for the dress, it may be necessary to join additional sections of fabric to the skirt panels at the hem. These are joined in the usual manner, with right sides of the fabric together and using a straight seam. Press open and finish in the same manner as the skirt seams.

(12) The two front skirt panels are joined at the seam marked A on the pattern. With right sides together, join the two panels, taking care to align the marks. Stitch and clip into the seam at the angled sections to help it lie flat.

11

Attached section at the skirt hem, from the inside.

10

Centre front bodice seam, from the inside.

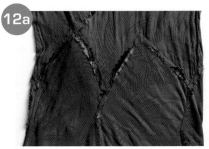

12a

Front skirt panel, seam detail on the inside.

(5) Pull the gathers up to match the measurement of the front bodice shoulder seam and secure by tying off the threads into a knot. With right sides together, join the front and back shoulder seams. Once stitched, finish the inside of the seam allowance by machining a second row of stitching 0.3cm (⅛in) above the seamline and trim any excess allowance to neaten.

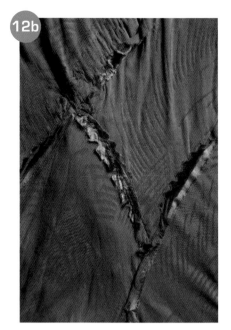

Front skirt, detail of clipped seam.

Finish by trimming the allowance using pinking shears.

(13) The back skirt panels are joined at the seam marked B on the pattern. With right sides together, join the two

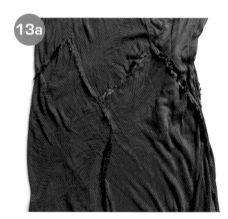

Back skirt panel, seam detail on the inside.

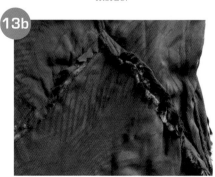

Back skirt, detail of finished seam.

panels, taking care to align the marks. Stitch and clip into the seam at the angled sections on the left panel to help it lie flat. Finish by trimming the allowance using pinking shears.

Joining the front and back skirt sections

(14) The skirt can now be joined at the side seams, marked C and D on the pattern. Use the marks on the pattern pieces to align both seams. Stitch the seams and finish by trimming the allowance using pinking shears. Clip into the seam at the angled section on D to help it lie flat.

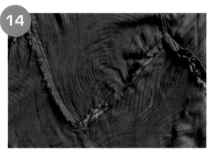

Clipped seam finish, on the inside.

Joining the bodice and skirt

(15) Begin by turning under the seam allowance around the bottom edge of the bodice. It will be necessary to clip into the angled sections and trim away excess fabric at the points in order to manipulate it and ensure the allowance lies flat and without bulk. Secure the fold by tacking into place. Working with right sides uppermost, position the bodice onto the skirt with the folded, lower edge of the bodice placed 1.2cm (½in) down from the raw edges of the skirt waistline.

(16) Due to the design of the dress, the right front bodice side seam is positioned adjacent to the skirt seam, rather than lined up with it.

(17) Once in position, it is advisable to tack the bodice and skirt together before stitching. Machine top-stitch the join, ensuring the stitching is neat and accurate, especially around the angled and pointed sections of the

Bodice side seam alignment on the right-hand side.

Top-stitching detail at the bodice and skirt join, right side.

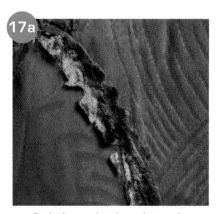

Pinked seam finish on the inside.

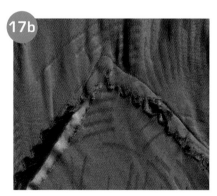

Seam detail at the points, on the inside.

bodice hem.

Once complete, remove all the tacking stitches and finish the inside seam allowance by trimming with pinking shears.

Finishing the skirt hem
(18) The skirt hem is finished with a delicate picot edge and this ensures the dress falls softly around the hem without extra bulk or weight. This was a popular finish in garments of this era and often found in high-end couture pieces. The beauty of this method of stitching and how it suits this style of dress is the fact that it creates a fine, lightweight hem that enhances the fluidity of shaping and cut. A picot edge is often used on circular-shaped hemlines and with fine fabrics as it creates extra fullness and swing on the fabric edge.

A true picot edge is created using a specialist machine and pressure foot, but a similar effect can be achieved using a regular sewing machine. The skirt hem can be created using a roll hemming pressure foot in conjunction with a zig-zag stitch. The fabric is run through the roll hemming foot in the usual manner but using a zig-zag stitch rather than a straight stitch in order to create the decorative finish.

It is always a good idea to test the stitching on an offcut of the dress fabric first, before attempting to tackle the dress itself and this is especially important with velvet fabrics. Try different stitch lengths and widths to gauge how the fabric will react. The original dress uses a very narrow, close stitch in order to give a fine finish to the skirt hem.

Alternatively, the raw edges of the

hem can be machined using a narrow, close zig-zag stitch and finished by trimming away any excess fabric fibres along the hem edge. If preferred, a narrow hand-rolled hem would be equally as effective.

Applying the front bodice neckline trim
(19) The ruched velvet trim at the neckline not only adds texture and embellishment to the dress, but also

gives weight and stability to the centre front bodice. Start at the left side of the neckline and lay a section of trim measuring approximately 29.5cm (11½in) long (allowing for turnings) along the neckline edge. Sew the trim onto the dress by hand, using rows of small, neat running stitches at each outer edge and through the centre, securing all the fabric layers together.
(20) At the shoulder, turn under a small hem of approximately 1–1.2cm (⅜–½in)

Skirt hem finish on the inside and right side.

Left side neckline trim attached, from the right side.

Left side neckline trim, finish detail on the inside.

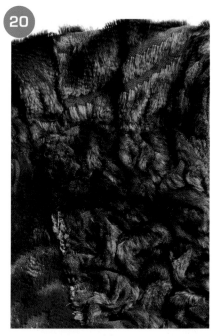

Left side neckline trim at the shoulder, from the right side.

Right side neckline trim attached, from the right side.

Right side neckline trim, finish detail on the inside.

Right side neckline trim at the waist.

and secure to the dress by hand using a slip-stitch.

(21) Repeat the process for the right side of the neckline, attaching a length of trim measuring approximately 48.5cm (19in) long (allowing for turnings) from the shoulder seam as before and following the angle of the centre front neckline; take it straight down to the point where the bodice

and skirt join. Both ends of the trim are finished in the same manner as previously described for the left side; remove any tacking stitches used for both trim pieces.

Creating and attaching the bow tails

(22) Begin by creating the bow tails, three small and one slightly larger. For each bow tail, take the pattern pieces and, with right sides together, stitch around the edges, leaving an opening

Bow tails at the pointed ends.

Bow tails at the gathered ends.

Bow tails in position on the skirt.

Bow tails complete and attached to the dress.

at the short, straight end, as indicated on the pattern. Take care to ensure the points are neat and sharp; once stitched, trim the seam allowances to 0.7cm (¼in), clipping across the ends of the points to reduce bulk. Turn the bow tails right sides out.

(23) At the unfinished end of each bow tail, sew a row of gathering stitches, either by hand or machine, and pull up to a measurement of 4cm (1½in). Secure the gathers by tying off the threads in a knot.

(24) Finally, the bow tails can be positioned and attached to the dress. Start by taking two of the smaller bow tails and the larger bow tail and place them one on top of the other in the order: small, large, small. Lay them marginally misaligned at the top edge, so that they will fall apart slightly when hanging from the dress and make sure all the pointed ends are facing the same way. Secure them together by hand using a few back- or running stitches, then attach to the dress at the base of the right side neckline trim, with pointed ends facing toward the centre font. Attach to the dress, through all the fabric layers, using a back-stitch, or slip-stitch if preferred; just ensure the stitching is sufficient to hold the bow tails securely.

The remaining bow tail can then be attached. Begin by turning under a small allowance (approximately 1.2cm/½in) at the gathered end and attach the folded edge over the others at the end of the bodice trim. Angle

this piece slightly toward the centre front of the dress and secure by hand, using a slip-stitch. This final bow tail should cover the raw edges of the others and hang down from the hip.

Back detail of blue devoré velvet evening dress.

STYLE GUIDE

A very thirties-looking evening gown, this velvet dress is a beautiful vibrant blue which would translate very well to the contemporary wearer. The slightly dropped waist and the bias cut of the skirt render this dress a comfortable and adaptable wear. The liberated woman could feel comfortable in a dress such as this, with its glamorous yet understated finish and its use of an interesting surface-decorated fabric. You might choose to create a shortened mid-length version of this dress, providing you with a more functional dress for everyday wear, perhaps paired with a boxy monochrome blazer to modernize.

Completed side bow on blue devoré velvet evening dress.

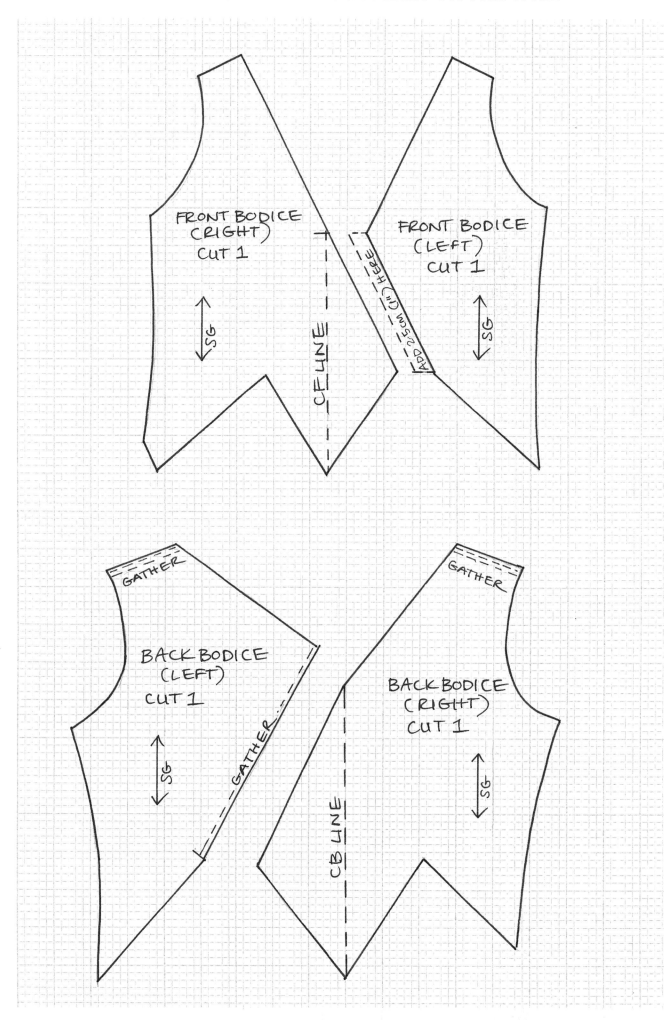

IMAGE 4440 PATTERN PAGE 2

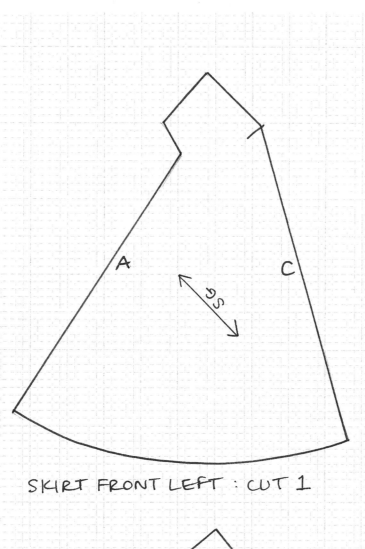

A

C

SG

SKIRT FRONT LEFT : CUT 1

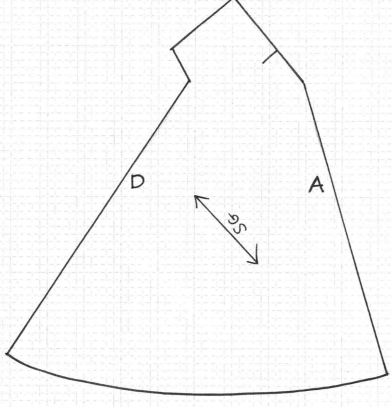

D

A

SG

SKIRT FRONT RIGHT : CUT 1

BLUE VELVET EVENING DRESS
SCALE 1:10 FOR ALL PATTERN PIECES ON THIS PAGE

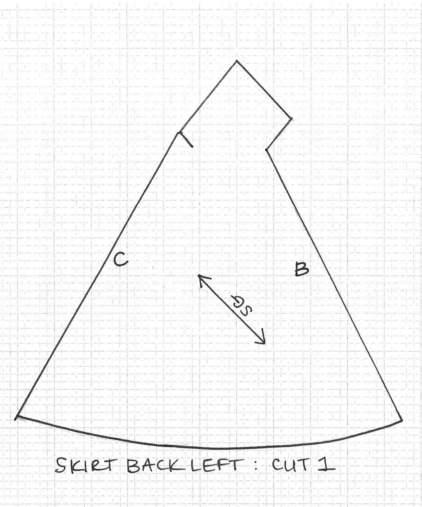

SKIRT BACK LEFT : CUT 1

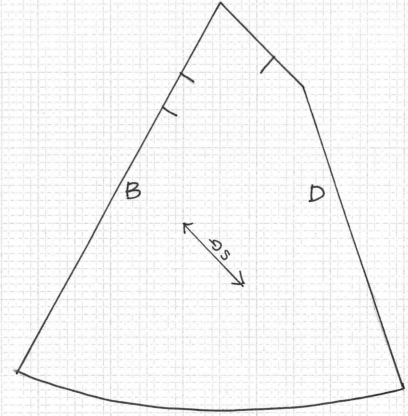

SKIRT BACK RIGHT : CUT 1

BLUE VELVET EVENING DRESS
SCALE 1:2 FOR ALL PATTERN PIECES ON THIS PAGE

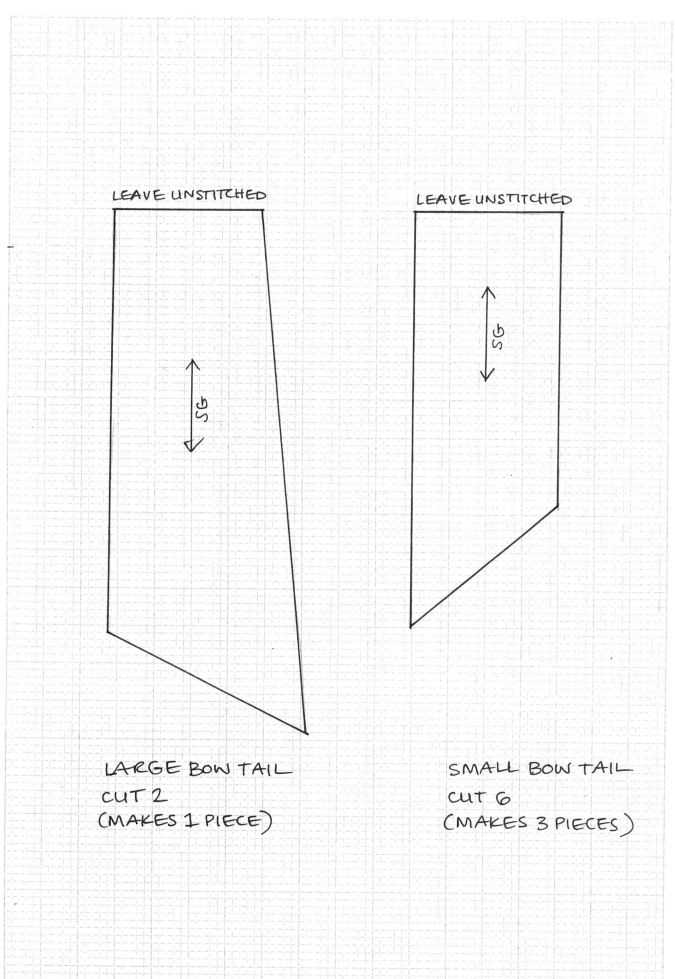

LEAVE UNSTITCHED

LEAVE UNSTITCHED

SG

SG

LARGE BOW TAIL
CUT 2
(MAKES 1 PIECE)

SMALL BOW TAIL
CUT 6
(MAKES 3 PIECES)

Evening Jacket

12

This simply styled yet sophisticated waist-length evening jacket is cut to create a subtle swing at the centre back; the front is an edge-to-edge design with no fastenings. The front panels of the jacket are shaped using a dart running down from the shoulder. Made from black silk velvet and with long sleeves, *the jacket is fully lined in ivory satin. The small shoulder pads give lift and add an element of structure to the otherwise relaxed fit.*

A soft rounded collar with narrow lapels give a tailored finish to the jacket, but it retains the soft styling in that the collar is not stiffened.

This elegant piece works perfectly in the choice of inky-black velvet, which imparts a gentle sheen, contrasting beautifully with the ivory lining. Any colour choice for the lining would work well against the classic black of the jacket.

Back of black velvet evening jacket.

Left: Black velvet evening jacket.

Instructions for Making Up
the Jacket

To start

Begin by cutting out all the pattern pieces for the jacket, adding seam and hem allowances, and set them aside. It is important to note that velvets have a definite direction of pile (nap) and each pattern piece must be placed with the pile running in the same direction. This will ensure there is no difference in shade/tone when the garment is sewn. Follow the guidelines for pressing velvet fabrics in the previous chapter on the blue velvet evening dress

Creating the front panel darts

(1) Take the front panel pattern pieces for both jacket and lining and, with right sides together, stitch the long shoulder darts, as indicated on the pattern. Press the lining darts toward the armholes and press the jacket darts as per the velvet pressing guidelines.

Joining the centre back panels

(2) Begin by joining the centre back seams on both the jacket and lining; with right sides together, stitch the seams. Next, join the side back panels on both the jacket and lining. With right sides together, stitch the seams marked A on the pattern. Finish the seams by pressing open and clip into seam A where necessary to ease.

Joining the front and back sections

(3) The front and back sections of both the jacket and lining can now be joined. With right sides together, join the shoulder and side seams, then stitch and press the seams open.

MEASUREMENTS

Bust: 94cm (37in)

Approximate dress size: UK 12, US 10, EU 42

FABRIC SUGGESTIONS AND NOTIONS

The ideal choice for this evening jacket is velvet and the options available are endless for colour, pattern and finish. A mid-weight fabric with good draping abilities will give the jacket the soft swing that gives its distinct styling; heavier velvets or those with a coarser pile (nap) will not hang as well. Straight-pile velvets will reflect the clean lines of the design, but equally as striking would be to use a velvet with a crushed pile to add texture and interest to the simple styling. Extra impact could be with the choice of satin lining, be it a colour contrast or use of a bold pattern. The satin fabric should, again, be of a mid-weight to match the jacket fabric.

Matching sewing thread

2 x 1.2cm (½in) shoulder pads

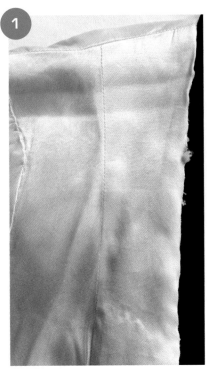

Back panel seam detail on the inside.

Front panel dart detail, from the inside.

Side seam detail on the inside.

Making up and attaching the under-collar

(4) Begin by joining the two sections that make up the under-collar at the centre back seam. With right sides together, stitch the seam then trim to approximately 1cm (⅜in). Next, take the completed under-collar section and, with right sides together, position the neckline edge of the collar onto the jacket neckline, aligning the centre back seams and the pointed end of the under-collar with the centre front line of the jacket.

Stitch, then trim the seam allowance to 0.7cm (¼in) and, following the velvet pressing guidelines, carefully press the seam up toward the top edge of the under-collar section. As an alternative, the seam can be tacked into position temporarily. If using this method, ensure the stitches are not too tight, as velvet fabrics mark easily.

Under-collar, from the underside.

Making up and attaching the front facing

(5) The front facing pattern pieces also act as the upper collar facing. Taking the two sections and with right sides together, join and stitch the centre back seam. Next, take the prepared facing and, with right sides together, position the facing around the jacket centre front lines and collar, aligning the centre back seams and the raw edges of the pattern pieces. Stitch, and then trim the seam allowance to 0.7cm (¼in). Turn the newly attached facing inside the jacket, with the seamline positioned along the edge of the garment.

(6) To keep the facing in place at the back neck, it can be secured between the shoulder seams by hand, using a prick stitch and working from the right side.

The remainder of the facing along the centre front can be secured temporarily using a tacking stitch. Make sure the fabric layers are lying flat and even and, to avoid marking the velvet, ensure the stitches are not too tight.

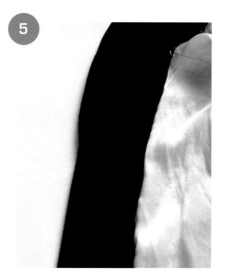

Front edge facing detail.

Under-collar stitching.

Finishing the jacket hem

(7) Start by turning up the single hem allowance and secure the raw edge to the jacket fabric by hand, using a herringbone stitch. Aim to make the stitches virtually invisible from the right side, with sufficient tension to hold the stitches in place but not so tight that they mark the velvet. Turn the bottom edges of the facing under and secure to the hem by hand, using a slip-stitch.

Facing at jacket hem.

Making up and inserting the sleeves

(8) Take the sleeve pattern pieces for both the jacket and lining and begin by joining the underarm seams. With right sides together, stitch the underarm seams and press open. Next and with right sides together, insert the sleeves into the prepared jacket and lining, ensuring the underarm and side seams are aligned and the centre

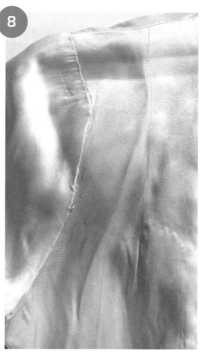

Detail of ease at armhole.

133

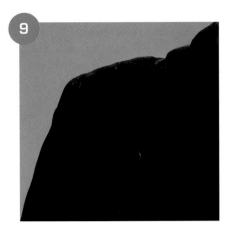

Shoulder pad inserted, from the right side.

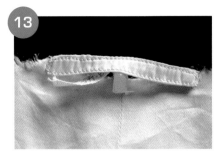

Back neck hanger strap.

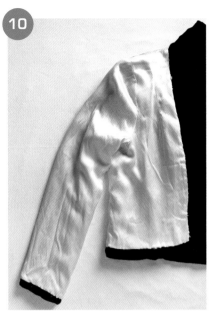

Jacket lining inserted.

Slip-stitching at jacket hem.

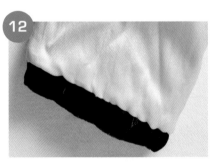

Slip-stitching at sleeve hem.

points of the sleeve heads are in line with the shoulder seams. Ease the sleeve heads around the shoulders, then stitch into position. Trim the seam allowances to approximately 1cm (⅜in) and clip into the curve of the armhole to allow ease of movement.

(9) The shoulder pads can now be inserted into the jacket. Position each pad with the flat end facing the neckline and the broader end inserted approximately 1.2cm (½in) into the sleeve head. Align the centre of the pad with the shoulder seam and secure by hand using a few back-stitches at the neckline point and around the pad at the armhole seam. The finished effect should give the shoulder a squared-off, tailored appearance.

Inserting the jacket lining

(10) Take the prepared lining and, with the wrong sides of the fabrics together, position the lining inside the jacket, pushing the sleeve linings into the sleeves. Line up the centre back neck seams, side and shoulder seams, then turn under the seam allowance around the back neck and down the centre front opening and secure to the jacket by hand, using a slip-stitch.

(11) Next, prepare the lining hem. To ensure the lining allows movement for the wearer and to avoid any sagging or pulling of the fabric on the right side, the lining hem should be turned under and then attached approximately 2.5cm (1in) above the bottom edge of the jacket hem and secured by hand, using a slip-stitch.

(12) The sleeve lining hems should be treated in the same manner as the jacket by turning under the hem allowance and positioning above the jacket sleeve hem, this time approximately 1.2cm (½in) above the bottom edge.

Creating the hanger strap

(13) The final step in making the jacket is to create the hanger strap that is positioned at the centre back neck. Begin

by cutting a section of the satin lining fabric, measuring approximately 9cm (3½in) long x 2.5cm (1in) wide. Turn under 0.3cm (⅛in) along each long edge and press to create sharp folds. Next, fold the fabric strip in half lengthways, so the two turned allowances are enclosed, then press again.

Machine edge-stitch along both long edges to secure and attach to the jacket lining at the centre back neck, aligning the centre of the strap with the centre back seam of the jacket lining. Turn under 0.7cm (¼in) at each end and secure to the lining by hand, using a slip-stitch. Make sure the stitches are small and tight to allow for the weight of the jacket to be supported.

EVENING JACKET
SCALE 1:5 FOR ALL PATTERN PIECES ON THIS PAGE

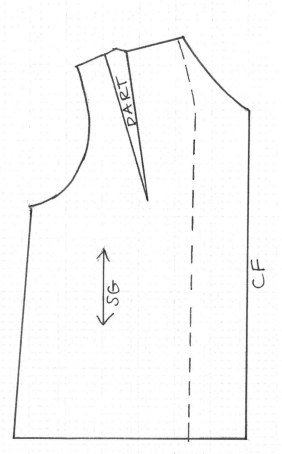

JACKET FRONT
CUT 2 : VELVET
CUT 2 : LINING
(TO MARK)

ADD 5CM (2") HEM
ALLOWANCE

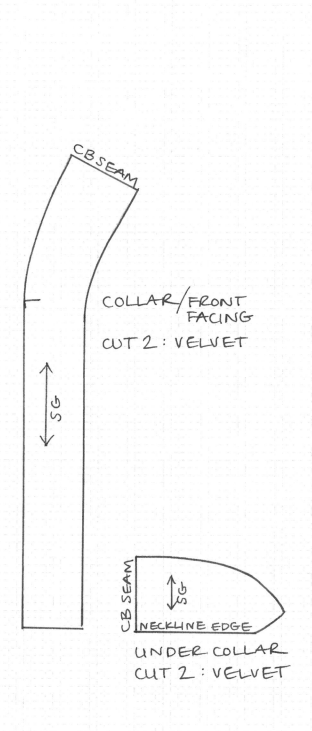

COLLAR/FRONT
FACING
CUT 2 : VELVET

UNDER COLLAR
CUT 2 : VELVET

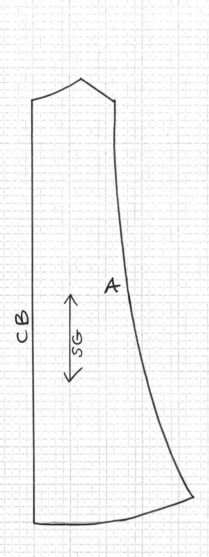

JACKET BACK

CUT 2 : VELVET

CUT 2 : LINING

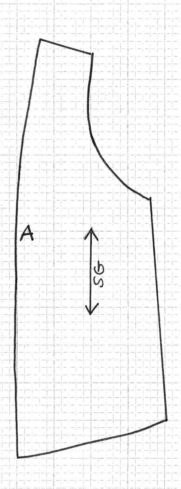

JACKET BACK
(SIDE PANEL)

CUT 2 : VELVET

CUT 2 : LINING

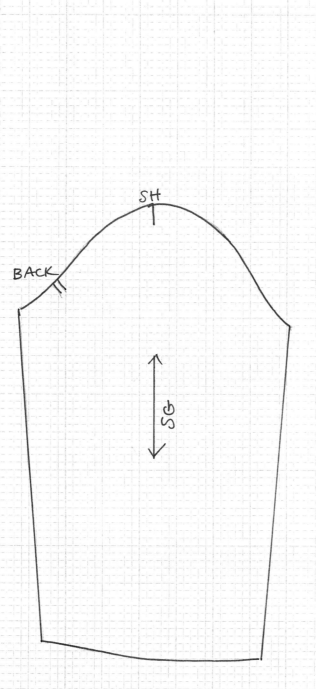

SH

BACK

SG

JACKET SLEEVE

CUT 2 : VELVET
CUT 2 : LINING

Coat

13

This stylish coat by Patrick Thomson Ltd of Edinburgh is a classic cocoon design typical of the era and is made from a heavyweight black wool felt. The coat has a wide, shawl-style collar with revers and moiré silk inserts at the lapel. Decorative faux buttonholes in Russia braid and silk-covered buttons decorate the lapels and give the coat a smart, military feel. The coat has dolman-style set-in sleeves of two-part construction with deep cuffs of a design complementary to the collar.

The tailored effect is further enhanced with top-stitching on the coat and around the cuffs and collar, yet the coat still retains a relaxed feel due to the loose fit. The coat is unlined and closes at the centre front with a single, large covered button and decorative frog fastener. An internal fastening tape, attached at the side seam, gives extra support and hold for the fastening.

Back of black coat.

Left: Black coat.

Instructions for Making Up the Coat

To start
Begin by cutting out all the pattern pieces for the coat, adding seam and hem allowances, and set them aside.

Creating the front panel darts
(1) Take the front coat panels and stitch the shoulder darts, as indicated on the pattern. Press open and trim to 0.3cm (⅛in).

Front panel dart on the inside.

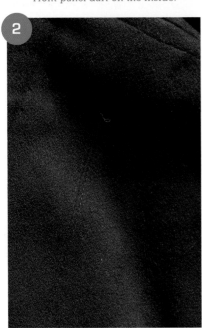

Dart top-stitching, from the right side.

(2) Working on the right side of the fabric, machine top-stitch along the length of the dart, on either side of the seam.

Joining the front and back coat panels
(3) With right sides together, join the front and back coat sections at the side and shoulder seams. Once stitched, press the seams open and trim the side seam allowances using pinking shears. **(4)** Trim the shoulder seams straight and to a measurement of 1cm (⅜in). Working from the right side, machine top-stitch either side of the seam, 0.7cm (¼in) out from the seamline.

Coat panel seam finish on the inside.

Top-stitching detail at shoulder, right side.

Making up and inserting the sleeves
(5) Begin by joining the front and back pattern pieces that make up the sleeve. With right sides together, join the sleeve along the central seam, as indicated on the pattern. Once stitched, trim the seam allowance to

Sleeve seam detail, from the right side.

1cm (⅜in) and press open. Working on the right side, machine top-stitch along either side of the central seam 0.7cm (¼in) out from the seamline.
(6) Now the underarm seam can be joined. With right sides together, stitch the seam and press open. Once the sleeves are complete, insert into the coat armholes, with right sides together and aligning the central sleeve seam with the shoulder seam, the underarm seam with the side seams and the underarm marks as indicated on the pattern. Stitch the sleeves into the coat, then press the allowance in toward the

Coat sleeve inserted.

main body of the coat. It will be necessary to clip into the allowance at the angles of the underarm marks. To finish, work from the right side and machine top-stitch around the armhole of the coat, 1cm (⅜in) out from the seamline.

Making up and attaching the cuffs
(7) Follow these instructions for both left and right cuffs. Begin by joining the cuff facing pattern pieces in the coat fabric and silk. Turn under the seam allowance around the upper and lower curved edges of the coat fabric facing and press to create a sharp,

Silk insert detail on cuff.

Top-stitching detail at back cuff.

folded edge. Clip into the curved edge to ease manipulation of the turning. Next, lay the coat fabric facing onto the silk, positioning the inner curved edge approximately 1.2cm (½in) in from the outer, curved raw edge of the silk.

Machine edge-stitch around the curved edge to secure and press to finish. Take the main cuff pattern piece and place the prepared silk insert section onto the cuff, in the position indicated on the pattern. Machine edge-stitch around the turned, upper curved edge of the insert to secure.
(8) Finish this stage by turning under the seam allowance along the upper edge and press to create a sharp fold. Machine edge-stitch the folded edge to secure, then measure down 2.5cm (1in) from the upper folded edge and machine a row of top-stitching around the cuff. Machine another row of stitching 0.3cm (⅛in) below this line and finally a third row another 0.3cm (⅛in) below the previous one. The cuff should now have a stitched upper edge, followed by three parallel rows of stitching below it.
(9) Join the two ends of the cuff by turning under the seam allowance at

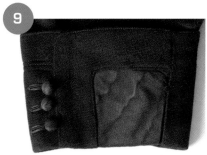

Cuff join, detail.

Cuff facing on reverse, detail.

Sleeve hem lining under the cuff.

the raw end and attaching it to the end with the decorative facing. Secure by hand using a slip-stitch. Turn under the seam allowance on the bottom edge of the cuff and press to create a sharp edge.

(10) Now attach the cuff facings. Working on the wrong side of the cuff, position the upper raw edge of the facing section approximately 1.2cm (½in) below the finished hem edge of the cuff. Attach to the cuff at the upper and lower edges by hand, using a slip-stitch.

(11) Before the cuff can be attached to the coat, the sleeve hem must be prepared. Begin by cutting two strips of silk or lining fabric to the measurement around the hem edge of the sleeve plus approximately 1.2cm (½in) allowance for joining, and measuring 5cm (2in) in width. Working

Sleeve hem lining, detail.

Position of the cuff on the sleeve.

Cuff attached at sleeve hem edge, detail.

from the right side of the sleeve hem, position the lining onto the sleeve and fold approximately 1.5cm (⅝in) over the raw edge of the hem and into the sleeve. Attach to the sleeve by hand, using an overcast stitch.

(12) The raw edge on the right side is attached in the same manner.

(13) The cuff can now be attached to the sleeve hem. Working from the right side of the sleeve, position the cuff so that the point where the curved upper edge of the decorative silk insert joins the upper edge of the cuff is aligned with the central sleeve seam.

(14) The hem edge of the cuff is positioned 0.7cm (¼in) below the sleeve hem in order to conceal it and both are joined by hand using a slip-stitch. Ensure the stitches are strong and secure.

Making up and attaching the collar and facings

(15) Start by preparing the lower front collar sections in the same manner as the cuffs, by turning under the seam allowances on the upper and lower curved edges of the outer facing pattern pieces. Press to create a sharp edge and clip into the curved areas.

where necessary to ease manipulation of the turning. Lay the piece onto the silk section, positioning the inner curved edge approximately 1.2cm (½in) in from the raw edge of the outer

Collar insert detail.

Lower collar, detail of reverse side.

Seam finish at the back collar.

Facing seam, back collar, detail.

Top-stitching on back collar, detail.

Collar attached to coat.

Secure temporarily using a tacking stitch.

(16) Next, take the front collar sections and, with right sides uppermost, position the lower front collar section onto the collar, aligning the outer curved edges. Machine edge-stitch around both curved outer edges, securing the lower front section to the collar.

(17) The back collar section can now be attached. With right sides together, join the two front collar sections to the back collar section. Stitch, then trim the seam allowance to approximately 1cm (⅜in) using pinking shears and press the seams open.

(18) Take the narrow facing sections for the front and back collar and, with right sides together, stitch, then trim the seam allowance to 0.7cm (¼in) and press open. The facing seams, as indicated on the pattern, are offset to reduce bulk around the collar edge once attached.

Working on the reverse side of the collar, position the facing with its outer raw edge positioned just below the outer folded edge of the collar and tack to secure temporarily. Turn the collar to work on the right side and machine edge-stitch around the outer edge of the upper front/back collar.

(19) Measure in 2.5cm (1in) from the outer edge and machine a row of top-stitching around the collar. Machine another row of stitching 0.3cm (⅛) below the previous row, followed by a third row another 0.3cm (⅛in) below the previous one. The collar should now have a stitched outer edge with three parallel rows of stitching below.

(20) Before the collar can be attached to the coat, the front facings must be prepared. On the wrong side of both facing sections, stitch a piece of heavyweight interfacing to stiffen, following the pattern piece for the facing. Next, turn under 0.7cm (¼in) along the inner raw edges, press to create a sharp edge, then machine edge-stitch to secure.

The collar and facings can now be joined. Begin by folding the centre front edge and back neck seam allowances to the inside of the coat and

Coat facing attached.

press to create a sharp fold. Working from the inside of the coat, position the long, straight raw edge of the collar onto the folded seam allowance and tack to secure temporarily. Now, take the front facing and, with the wrong sides uppermost, lay the raw edges of the centre front line onto the centre front of the coat, positioning the facing 1.2cm (½in) in from the edge.

(21) Stitch to secure the facing and collar onto the coat, then turn the front facing to the inside of the coat and press. Tack to secure temporarily.

Finishing the hem
(22) Begin by turning up a 1.2cm (½in) hem, press to create a sharp fold then tack to secure temporarily. Next, cut a 1.8cm (¾in) wide strip of the coat fabric to the measurement along the coat hem, plus an extra 0.7cm (¼in) to join. Working on the inside of the coat, lay the strip flat and position it around the hem, covering the turned allowance and folding under 0.7cm (¼in) at each end.

(23) Machine edge-stitch along the bottom edge of the hem and 2.5cm (1in) up onto the centre front facing to secure. Finally, working on the right side of the coat, machine top-stitch the centre front, collar and hem 2.5cm (1in) in from the outer edges. Start at a

Hem facing, from the inside.

Top-stitching detail on the coat.

shoulder seam and stitch in a continuous line around the coat. Remove all the tacking stitches and press to finish.

Attaching the back neck facing
(24) Begin by turning under the seam allowance round the entire pattern piece and press to create a defined edge. Working on the inside of the coat, place the facing onto the back neck, aligning at the centre points, and secure all the way around by hand, using a slip-stitch.

Back neck facing on the inside.

Attaching the decorative fastenings and embellishments
(25) For the cuffs, take three sections of Russia braid measuring 5cm (2in) in length and fold in half to create the illusion of a bound buttonhole. Position on the cuff at the marks indicated on the pattern, with the raw end at the vertical join on the cuff. Secure the

Cuff buttons in position.

Collar buttons in position.

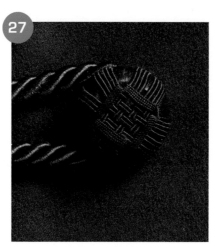

Passementerie button.

braid at each end by hand, using a few back-stitches. Attach a covered button at the raw end of each braid section.
(26) For the collar, attach the Russia braid using the same method as the cuffs, following the marks indicated on the pattern. Attach a hook and eye to secure the collar at the centre front. Sew the hook just inside the right centre front edge of the collar, 11.5cm (4½in) down from the top point of the silk insert. On the left side of the collar, attach the corresponding eye at the same measurement down.
(27) The large, decorative button is of passementerie style. Passementerie is the creation of a decorative trim using braid, cord, embroidery or beading and is still a popular form of embellishment today. Attach the button to the coat on the left front panel, at the mark indicated on the pattern, and sew using a small piece of the coat fabric behind the button on the inside to strengthen.
(28) The decorative frog fastener is positioned on the right front panel, at the angle indicated on the pattern, leaving one loop free to secure across to the button. Secure the fastener to the coat by hand-sewing round the outer edges, using a slip-stitch.

Frog fastener in position.

Attach inside tape closure
(29) The final step is to attach the tape fastener inside the coat. At the right side seam, attach the tape approximately 62cm (24½in) up from the bottom of the coat hem; fold under a 1.2cm (½in) turning and sew it

Fastening tape positioned inside the coat.

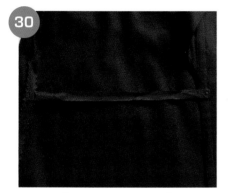

Fastening tape secured.

securely onto the seam by hand using an overcast stitch.

(30) At the opposite end of the tape, turn under 1.2cm (½in) and attach one part of the press stud. Attach the other part of the press stud to the right side of the centre front edge of the left coat panel, approximately 62cm (24½in) up from the bottom of the coat hem.

Collar detail of black coat.

Frog fastener on black coat.

STYLE GUIDE

A heavy winter coat is an essential for any capsule collection. The frogging detail on this coat would make for a beautiful addition to any winter coat you might want to adapt. The length of this coat and the three-quarter-length sleeves create an elegant sophisticated look that would work really well with some wide-knit accessories such as a chunky scarf. The two different fabrics utilized in the coat provide some interest around the collar and lapels. This coat could be worn with any ensemble of day or evening wear, perhaps paired with jeans and trainers for a casual winter look or with heels and a fitted dress or jumpsuit for an evening look. The beauty of a coat such as this is its versatility combined with the lift provided by the minimal but effective detailing.

Upper part of coat front.

Cuff detail on black coat.

COAT
SCALE 1:5 FOR ALL PATTERN PIECES ON THIS PAGE

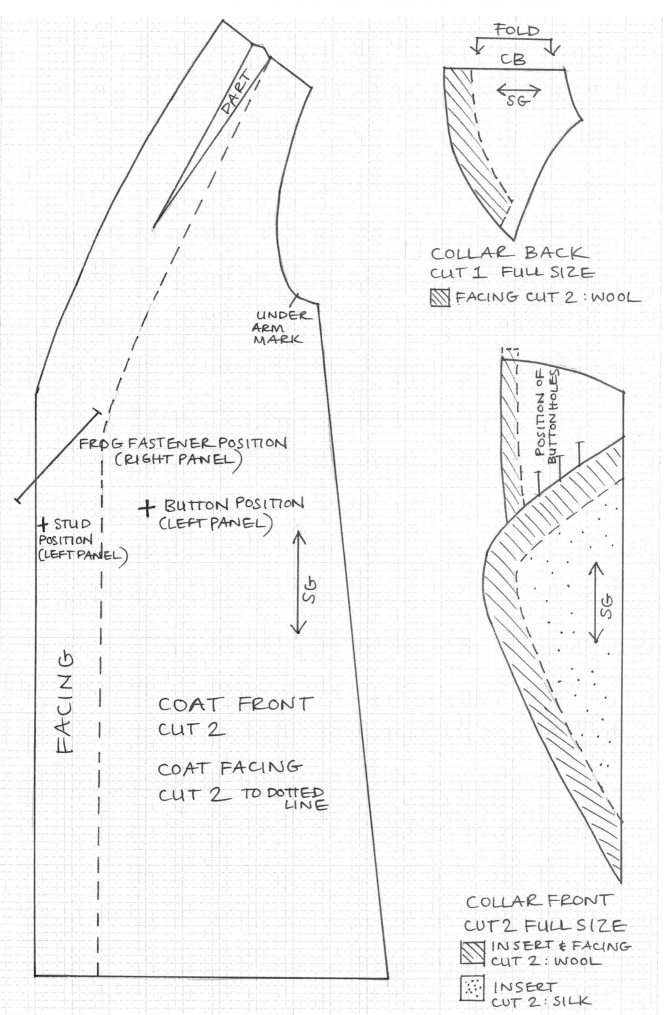

DART

UNDER ARM MARK

FROG FASTENER POSITION (RIGHT PANEL)

+ BUTTON POSITION (LEFT PANEL)

+ STUD POSITION (LEFT PANEL)

FACING

SG

COAT FRONT CUT 2

COAT FACING CUT 2 TO DOTTED LINE

FOLD

CB

SG

COLLAR BACK CUT 1 FULL SIZE

FACING CUT 2 : WOOL

POSITION OF BUTTON HOLES

SG

COLLAR FRONT CUT 2 FULL SIZE

INSERT & FACING CUT 2 : WOOL

INSERT CUT 2 : SILK

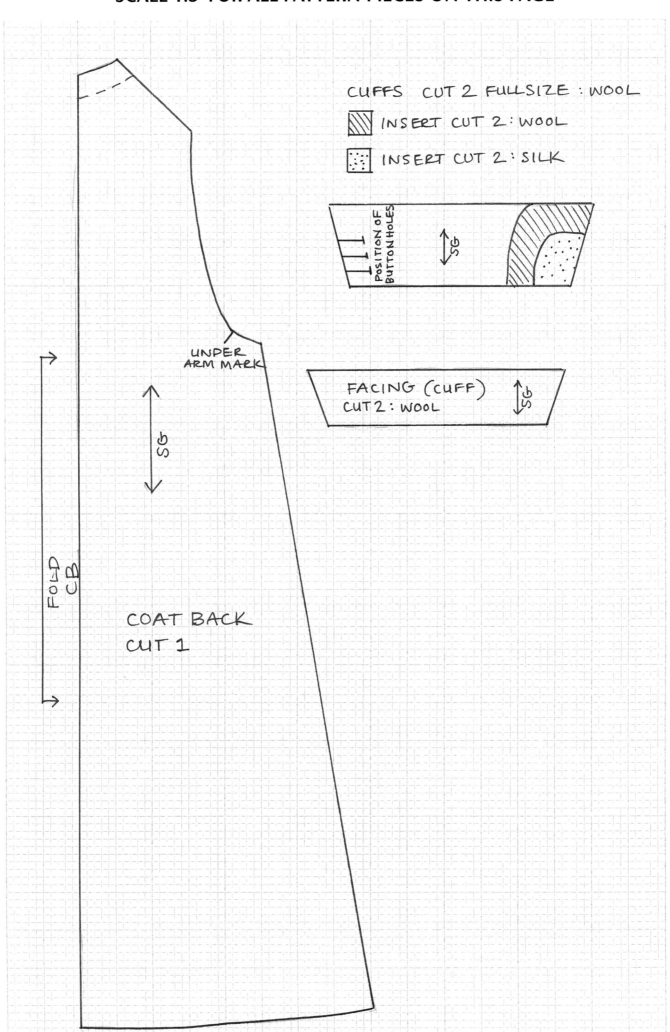

CUFFS   CUT 2 FULLSIZE : WOOL

INSERT CUT 2 : WOOL

INSERT CUT 2 : SILK

POSITION OF BUTTONHOLES

SG

FACING (CUFF)
CUT 2 : WOOL

SG

UNDER ARM MARK

SG

FOLD CB

COAT BACK
CUT 1

COAT
SCALE 1:5 FOR ALL PATTERN PIECES ON THIS PAGE

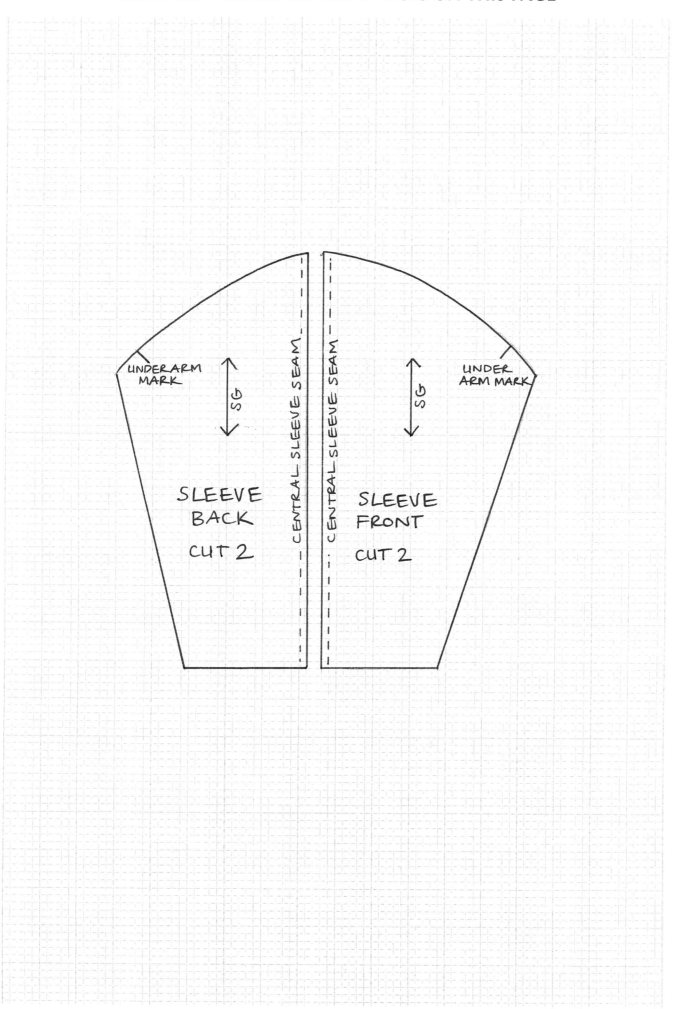

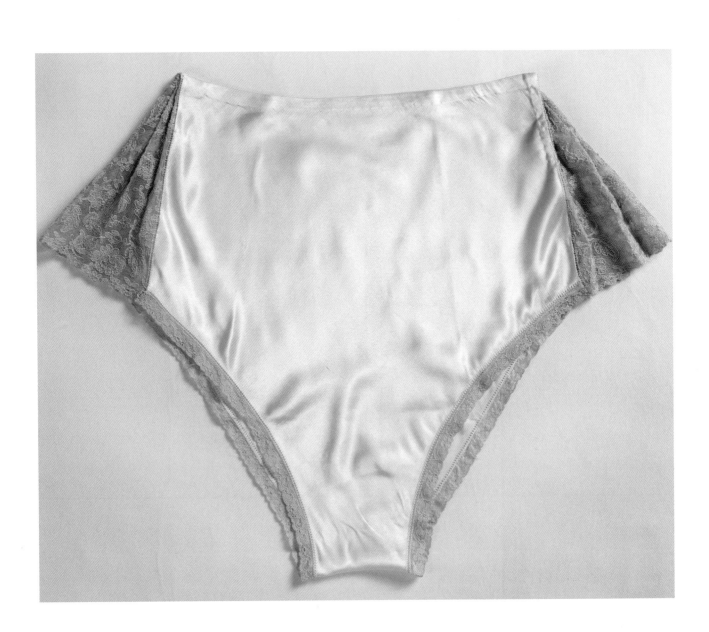

Caring for your Garment

14

As a museum service we are dedicated to the preservation and care of our dress and textiles collections, and the garments that make up our 1930s collection pieces require extra attention due to their fine fabrics and bias cuts. Each garment is considered individually for its condition, fabric type and styling before a decision is made as to how it will be stored; the long-term preservation of these garment types is dependent on several factors.

Even before considering the type of packaging to use to store your garment it is essential to make sure that it is clean before it is stored away in the wardrobe or drawer. Clothing is made to be worn and the accumulation of stains, dirt or debris being absorbed into the fibres of the fabric, if not attended to, could prove detrimental to the stability of the garment in the long term. Organic stains, such as sweat, food and beverages, are also an instant attractant to insect pests and, if left unchecked, have the potential to cause irreversible damage to the garment.

Certain types of dirt and staining can also, if the environmental conditions are unstable, attract moisture which can lead to problems with mould growth, and some of the garments in our collection have the brown spots known as 'foxing' which are indicative of a damp storage environment.

As well as being clean, the fabric of the garment should ideally have as few creases as possible, especially with fine fabrics such as silk or chiffon. Creases can break down to become irreparable splits, usually accelerated by exposure to ultraviolet and visible (daylight) light sources. Throughout the life of a garment it will have been exposed to high levels of light so it is worth periodically checking the condition of your garment for any splits or tears that may have occurred; the sooner these are fixed, the more stable your garment will continue to be.

Cleaning the types of fabrics that have been used to create the garments described in this book should be carried out by a specialist professional, as they will require differing cleaning techniques and the cleaning solution suitable for one fabric type may not be suitable for another. There are also the embellishments to consider too, such as beading or embroidered details, which can be damaged in the cleaning process. It is worth taking the time to source a suitable cleaning company and going on recommendation is always a good idea. Once your garment has been cleaned, leave it unwrapped in a cool room and away from direct sunlight for a couple of days to ensure that any residual vapours have left it.

At the museum we never wet-clean the pieces in our collection for reasons of fragility and because the dyes used in the fabric or any pattern/print could be fugitive and might disperse if moistened. If it is absolutely necessary and it would be to the detriment of the piece if it remained soiled, there are specialist conservators whom we would approach to deal with this type of cleaning as they have the knowledge, training and equipment to treat textiles. However, making your garment from new gives you greater choice; as long as cleaning is carried out carefully, there is no reason why your beautifully crafted vintage-style piece should not give you pleasure for many years to come.

For example, the lingerie set could be gently hand-washed with a mild detergent and then air-dried flat. Just make sure not to wring fine or delicate fabrics, as this could distort the fibres. Either gently and evenly squeeze out the water or, if the fabric is robust enough, place the garment through a gentle spin cycle on the washing machine. Always check that fasteners such as buttons and hooks are secure. Modern metal hooks should not be prone to corroding and are fine to put through a gentle wash. Carefully reshape whilst the garment is still damp and, if necessary, dry it flat.

Storage is the next question to consider and it wholly depends on the choice of fabric and the cut and construction of your garment as to whether it can be safely stored on a hanger. Hanging a garment certainly takes up less storage space than a box, but not all pieces are suitable to be stored in this way. The type of fabric used and the construction of the garment need to be considered; stretch fabrics or a dress cut on the bias, such as the black satin evening gown in the book, will gradually stretch and distort over time if placed on a hanger. The weight of the garment, be it the result of fabric type or volume, should be considered too; a heavy coat, for example, will have a considerable amount of strain placed on the shoulders if it is to be hung but, certainly in the home setting, it would be impractical to store it in a box. Investing in good-quality hangers of the correct size and strength for the garment (preferably padded ones using inert materials) will not only help to retain its shape but also ease any strain.

A padded hanger is always recommended for storing historic

Left: High-leg silk satin knickers.

garments and at the museum we adapt hangers to suit the differing requirements of the variety of garment types we care for in our collections. Wooden hangers are usually used but are carefully covered and padded to ensure that no substances such as acids in the wood permeate through to the stored garment. They are also often cut down at the ends to accommodate a narrow shoulder, for example. The materials used are inert, such as polyester wadding and unbleached calico cotton. The aim is to ensure that the hanger is soft and supportive of the shoulders and just into the sleeve, without putting any strain on the garment.

If the decision has been made that the garment can safely be stored on a hanger, it is important that the right type of cover is chosen to give sufficient protection. A good garment cover should be lightweight yet robust enough to protect the piece inside. Fabrics such as unbleached cotton are ideal and the closure should be with tie fastenings or a zip, never a hook and loop fastening as delicate areas of the garment could catch when being removed from the cover. If purchasing a garment cover, ensure the fabric is breathable, secures well and is not dyed. Avoid using a plastic cover, as plastic will degrade and potentially emit chemicals that could permeate the fabric.

Flat storage may prove the best and safest option for your garment and storing in a drawer is certainly suitable for the underwear and, if large and long enough, the bias-cut evening dresses described in the book. Make sure, if storing in a wooden drawer, that the garment is not placed in direct contact with the wood, for the same reasons as described in the use of hangers. Drawer liners are a good idea, but avoid the perfumed types or any with strong colours or patterns which could be transferred to the fabric. Interleaving with acid-free tissue not only protects the garment, but can help to avoid the creasing that occurs when items of clothing are stored together and this would be essential if storing a larger piece in a drawer. The secret to any good packaging is to create enough support, yet not fill the box or drawer so full of layers of tissue that the garment is overwhelmed with its volume. Create enough layers of support to keep the garment safe and supported, but ensure that it can also be accessed and checked without over-handling or searching through vast quantities of tissue paper. As with boxes, never over-stuff a drawer with clothing items as this will not only cause crushing but also provide a great hiding place for pests and could encourage the growth of mould. The room in which you store your garment should be of even temperature, preferably cool and dark. Considering how you store your finished garment will ensure it remains in pristine condition. It is also good practice to keep wardrobes and drawers clean and dust-free. Inspect the contents periodically for changes in your garment's condition, to check the state of the packing materials and to see if any insect pests have found their way in.

And finally, don't forget to wear your garment with pride; after all, you made it!

Conclusion

15

This book is designed to act as a guide and a source of inspiration to anyone hoping to make, or who has made, a thirties-inspired capsule collection wardrobe or an individual thirties-inspired garment. This book is founded on original garments from within a museum collection, allowing the authors to fully engage with and reinterpret these garments for the reader to utilize and learn from. By using these patterns and instructions as the basis either for your own adaptation or for recreating one of the garments exactly, the outcome will be a demonstration of your patience, ability and creativity. With plenty of time and the correct skills, this book will allow you to create an elegant vintage garment that celebrates the beauty and delicacy of the female form. This will be a creation inspired by a garment that was worn in a time of crisis and instability, but one that signifies the fruitful and innovative nature of design and fashion at that time.

This book has allowed us to explore the museum collections in a new way, discovering details we had previously not seen, encouraging us to look at them in a different way and to share them with a new and dedicated audience. The importance of visually and mentally picking apart these garments in order to understand how they have been constructed has opened up new avenues for us to explore, shedding some light on the ways in which patterns were cut in the 1930s and the interesting and intricate dressmaking and sewing techniques that were used. This experience, in conjunction with in-depth research into the historical context and fashion produced at this time, has provided us with a greater understanding of how we can utilize these historic skills and ideas, translating them to contemporary dressmaking.

The opportunity to make your own thirties-inspired garment is a truly creative and inspirational one. It allows you to redefine your own unique look, one that is grounded in an age of elegance and sophistication. The variety of the garments included within this book, and the information on what could have been worn during the thirties, provides you with a huge pool of styles to choose from when selecting which garment you will recreate or reinterpret. You can create an entire thirties capsule collection or one that is merely inspired by certain 1930s features, or you could even create just an individual garment to incorporate into your look: the choice is yours. All the garments in the book can be worn with other pieces or accessories from your own wardrobe, which ensures that what you create is adaptable and versatile – an essential in the contemporary woman's wardrobe.

Follow the instructions carefully when creating your garment, as the fine fabrics utilized in the original garments are incredibly delicate and, at times, difficult to work with. Do not be put off by the difficulty in this venture, take your time and persevere with the fabric as the final product will be worth it. The nature of fabrics such as silk and chiffon are designed to flow gracefully over the body, which requires patience when trying to manipulate them through a sewing machine. The bias-cut technique is one that will be new for some; however, the shape and silhouette you can create with this cut is essential to a thirties-inspired garment. Be prepared to get to know the fabric, feel it, see how it moves and falls as this understanding will help you in controlling and building a shape with it.

The fashion history explored in this book has provided us with a greater understanding of how 1930s clothing developed and evolved over time. This understanding and appreciation of the decade and its context was essential to providing a clearer and more cohesive step-by-step guide on how to create your own thirties-inspired garment. Having this understanding of thirties fashion and its ethos grounded the patterns in experience and reliability, ensuring the design features and techniques were considered throughout.

The socio-political context of the thirties was one of constant flux and crisis. The Wall Street Crash of 1929 caused a global economic crisis that shook the world. This economic downturn had such an impact that the Great Depression shortly followed, in which financial stability was hard to sustain for most of society. This was abruptly followed by the declaration of WWII, an event that would leave a blot on the face of Western history forever. It was hard to envisage a way in which the arts could flourish; however the 1930s proved to be a fertile environment for creativity and innovation that would see fashion design blossom.

The styles of the 1930s showed great change when compared to the preceding Jazz Age. The streamlining of the silhouette would dominate in this decade, creating a new platform on which to highlight and celebrate the female form. The shift from loosely fitting tubular flapper dresses to the elegant figure-hugging column dresses of the thirties demonstrates a refocus of the emancipation and liberation of the female body. Although liberating in its loosely fitting shapeless design, the twenties flapper dress still required a tightly fitting girdle designed to restrict the wearer's body into a smooth tubular shape. This, in its essence, was similar to the shackles of the Edwardian corset such women were so keen to escape from. The 1930s, in particular the couturier Madeleine Vionnet, pushed this one step further by freeing the body of all restrictive and shaping undergarments. The body was now free of these confinements.

The 1930s garment had a natural waistline, and was soft and fluid. The adoption of the bias cut by Madeleine Vionnet popularized this method with many other designers, embedding this new silhouette firmly within the style zeitgeist of the decade. The revival of classicism saw this streamlined Grecian shape emerge from fabric that was elegantly draped around the body. Followers of the bias cut and the work of Vionnet could now create a fit and shape that was not possible when cutting fabric in the traditional way of using the straight grain as a guide. Vionnet was both a highly skilled craftswoman and a couturier, treating the fabric as a medium to be moulded and manipulated. This required a level of skill, appreciation and understanding of fabric like no one else had demonstrated, which for many rendered her the most influential couturier of the twentieth century.

The role of Paris in the thirties was similar to the role it plays today in our contemporary fashion industry. As an epicentre of taste making and trend setting, Paris was the most influential and important city at the time. The world took note of the new styles and changes in silhouette that were coming out of Paris, rendering the couturiers within it some of the most influential of all time. Parisian couture houses were the most active and inspirational, relied upon by manufacturers from around the world to set the tone for fashion design and creation. Even in times of crisis such as the 1929 Crash, when the Parisian fashion market was shaken, the couturiers still moved with the changing environment and developed inventive ways in which they could survive and flourish. The influence of

Parisian couture on the burgeoning ready-to-wear market is just one example of this.

Given the economic crisis that many were greatly affected by, the more affordable ready-to-wear market boomed, allowing more women from all social classes and backgrounds to wear fashionable clothing. The ready-to-wear market essentially democratized fashion, something that created the clothing industry we know today. The ability to afford fashionable clothing was now ensured even in times of financial crisis. The catalogue shopping industry also developed as a result of the necessity to work or seek employment during these difficult financial times. Catalogue shopping allowed very busy working women the option to undertake their shopping from the comfort of their own home, choosing from a hugely increased variety and selection of fashion and goods.

The couture industry also ensured its sustainability by offering semi-made garments that required finishing and sewing of seams at home by the purchaser. This allowed more women to wear simplified and less fussy versions of high fashion garments, once again demonstrating the availability of fashion to more of society at this time. The simplified silhouette and the minimal decoration of fashionable garments at this time made this process of design even easier for the couture houses offering such products.

The 'Golden Age' of design could also be considered the 'Golden Age' of Hollywood. The impact cinema and the film industry would have on fashion and vice versa could not be underestimated. At first the Hollywood costume produced for film was considered gaudy and vulgar by the Parisian couturiers; however, the mutual benefits these two industries could experience rendered them kindred spirits. The Hollywood designers found Paris and its fashion industry a vital source of inspiration, although they also used the platform of film to set many of their own trends. For the average woman, the cinema and

the films being produced in Hollywood provided the perfect source of inspiration, given the alluring glitz and glamour associated with it. The silver screen and the associated advertising campaigns sponsored by brand manufacturers encouraged the spread of thirties fashion around the USA and beyond.

The new following of the Art Moderne movement saw the sleek silhouette develop even further, with couturiers now paring back and simplifying their garments in order to minimize clutter. The lack of ornamentation and an adherence to only subtle surface decoration created a new emphasis on the cut and fall of the fabric. The back of the garment and the wearer were now a focal point for couturiers. Elegantly draping cowl necks, loose bows and diamanté back jewellery all highlighted the graceful curves of the body and the defined muscles of the idealized female back. This newly directed focus on the female form and the lack of shaping and smoothing undergarments increased the need for physical fitness in order to develop and maintain this idealized figure.

Activewear was pushed further than ever before in the thirties, with designers such as Patou and Chanel developing garments that were both functional and comfortable as well as fashionably chic. The use of jersey rendered Chanel's designs unique, and ideal for physical activity and relaxing. The growth of sporting events and the growing opportunities to attend and partake in them rendered activewear a staple element of the thirties wardrobe. The enhanced liberation of women allowed them to partake in sports at a professional level, and the developments in sportswear made this possible. It was no longer appropriate for an athlete to struggle in layers of heavy fabric and restrictive corsetry. The enhanced motion and function of activewear and sportswear was revolutionary and would change the way designers approached these garments.

Fabric innovations greatly improved

the design of swimwear, allowing for better fitting and stylish bathing suits. The introduction of Lastex allowed bathing suits that stayed fitted to the skin rather than sagging when wet. The incorporation of figure-enhancing features such as floating bras and side-smoothing seams created glamorous and elegant swimwear designed to be worn on the chicest of beaches in popular resort destinations. The desire to achieve a suntan was enhanced by swimsuits designed to maximize exposure and to minimize lines, through releasable and removable straps. The development of the resort saw the development of the associated fashions. It was now popular to spend summers in beautiful locations, entertaining friends, lounging on beaches and attending evening events that all required an elegant and

sophisticated resort wardrobe. This wardrobe was also necessary to walk the decks of the glorious ocean liners that were now populating the seas. Style on board was considerably more relaxed than on land, which saw the loosening of morals and the acceptance of more skin on show and the wearing of trousers by women.

With such an interesting and innovative fashion, social and political history, it is easy to understand why the 1930s has intrigued writers, historians and fashion designers today. The construction of clothing in the 1930s changed the course of style, with a new direction that embraced change and liberation. In our current society, the 1930s has so much to offer the modern woman; whether it is a sleek and elegant silhouette that you are seeking or a representation of a new age of

independence, the thirties is the place to source your ideas. We use our clothing and the way we wear it to express our identity, through the image we choose to construct and present to the world. You have a wonderful opportunity to create your own garments to express your personality, identity and style in a manner that is befitting of your tastes, your figure and your dressmaking skills.

In the age of both crisis and elegance, the 1930s brought with it a timeless and feminine silhouette, trailblazing fabric innovations and a streamlined aesthetic that have stood the test of time. With the dedication, commitment and creativity to constructing a thirties-inspired garment, you will bring this remarkable era back to life.

Glossary

Chiffon: A very thin silk or nylon cloth that is translucent and lightweight.

Cotton: A soft fluffy fibre that surrounds the seed pod of the cotton plant. The fibres go through many preparatory processes to make a yarn which is then spun into thread for sewing or into a huge variety of cloth products.

Crêpe: A thin fabric with an uneven surface which can be made from wool, silk or cotton.

Crêpe de Chine: A soft and thin crêpe usually made of silk. It is sometimes made with a satin backing.

Devoré velvet: A velvet fabric with a raised pattern that is created by disintegrating some of the pile using chemicals: it is sometimes referred to as 'burnout'.

Georgette: A thin silk or cotton crêpe fabric with a matt finish. If it has a crinkled finish it is referred to as georgette crêpe.

Lastex: An elastic rubber yarn sheathed by rayon, silk, nylon or cotton threads. It is made into fabrics that stretch and recover easily.

Lingerie net/tulle: A soft fine nylon or silk cloth which is similar to net. It is unusual in having a hexagonal mesh.

Moiré silk: A silk fabric with a wavy patterned finish that resembles water, hence its other name: watered silk. The finish is produced by passing the fabric between heavy rollers under heat.

Nylon: A strong flexible synthetic fabric. It is a class of synthetic polyamide material made by copolymerizing dicarboxylic acids with diamines. Textiles made from nylon are strong and elastic.

Pongee silk: A thin plain-weave silk fabric, originally from China, that has a nubbed effect from the characteristic slubs of wild silk. It is often left in its natural honey colour but can be dyed. There are cotton or rayon versions, but these do not necessarily come in the same natural colour.

Rayon: A smooth fabric made from cellulose or wood pulp, which is extruded through jets to create yarn.

Satin: A smooth, shiny cloth made from silk. It is closely woven to show much of the warp and this gives it a lustrous, glossy appearance.

Silk: A substance produced by silkworms who spin thread to create their cocoons in preparation for pupation. The silk can be unwound and processed and made into sewing thread or woven into smooth fine fabrics that are soft and lustrous.

Stretch lace: A delicate cloth with very open patterns created by interlaced threads; the stretch version incorporates man-made fibres to give elasticity.

Velvet: A woven, tufted fabric used in clothing manufacture and upholstery. It is distinctive by its luxurious, soft feel. The fabric can be woven in silk, cotton or synthetic fibres and has a short, dense pile or nap, which is formed by evenly distributed cut threads.

Wool: A fine, soft and often curly or wavy hair that forms the coat of an animal, usually a sheep or goat. When spun into yarn and made into cloth the resulting fabric is notable for its warmth and springiness.

Acknowledgements

We would like to thank Tessa Hallmann once again for sharing her time with us, supporting all the work that we do, and for her beautiful photography. Her dedication to capturing the perfect photograph has allowed us to showcase these beautiful garments by emphasizing their construction, elegance and story. On behalf of us and them, thank you, Tessa. Secondly, we would like to thank Iona Farrell for her innate ability to simply know when we needed some encouragement, and for her enthusiasm, excitement and passion for all things museums.

Ciara: I would like to thank my partner Oran, my father Paul and my sister Eavann for their love and support during the writing process of this book. Oran's unfaltering belief in my ability to get it done was hugely encouraging. I would also like to thank my dearest friend Mollie for her continued cheerleading when the pages were blank, and to Jade for being the perfect distraction when they weren't. Lastly, I would like to thank my co-author and partner in crime Claire, whose determination and appetite for a challenge makes me ask – What's next?

Claire: I would personally like to thank Tessa Hallmann, whose patience was endless when I asked her if she would mind taking 'just one more shot' for the step-by-step instructions – there were hundreds! Her stunning images bring the clothes to life and the book would not have been the same without her input. Thank you to Tamar Hicks, who is trying out the patterns for me and whose passion for historic dress and textiles is inspiring. And of course to my co-author Ciara – I couldn't have done it without you ... again!

Bibliography

Arnold, J., *Patterns of Fashion*, Vol. 2 (Macmillan, 1977)

Arnold, R., *The American Look: Fashion and the Image of Women in 1930s and 1940s New York* (I.B. Tauris, 2008)

Behnke, A., *The Little Black Dress and Zoot Suits: Depression and Wartime Fashions from the 1930s to the 1950s* (Twenty First Century Books, 2011)

Berry, S., *Screen Style: Fashion and Femininity in 1930s Hollywood* (University of Minnesota Press, 2000)

Blum, D., *Shocking! The Art and Fashion of Elsa Schiaparelli* (Philadelphia Museum of Art, 2004)

Blum, S., *Everyday Fashions of the Thirties: As Pictured in Sears Catalogs* (Dover, 1987)

Chadwick, W., *The Modern Woman Revisited: Paris Between the Wars* (Rutgers University Press, 2003)

Costantino, M., *The 1930s (Fashions of a Decade)* (Chelsea House, 2006)

Cowling, E., Mundy, J., *On Classical Ground: Picasso, Leger, de Chirico and the New Classicism 1910–1930* (Tate Gallery, 1990)

De la Haye, A., *Chanel: The Couturiere at Work* (V&A Publications, 1997)

Divita, L., 'Historical Influences on Contemporary Fashion Design', in Joanne B. Eicher and Phyllis G. Tortora, eds, Berg *Encyclopedia of World Dress and Fashion: Global Perspectives* (Berg, 2010)

Elia, A., 'The Wardrobe of the Modern Athlete: Activewear in the 1930s', in Mears and Boyer (eds), *Elegance in the Age of Crisis: Fashions of the 1930s* (Yale University Press, 2014)

Ewing, W., *Edward Steichen: In High Fashion: The Condé Nast Years 1923–1937* (Thames & Hudson, 2008)

Fiell, C., Dirix, E., *1930s Fashion: The Definitive Sourcebook* (Goodman Fiell, 2012)

Golbin, P., *Madeleine Vionnet* (Rizzoli International, 2008)

Kirke, B., *Madeleine Vionnet* (Chronical Books, 1998)

Lehmann, U., *Tigersprung: Fashion in Modernity* (MIT Press, 2000)

Mackrell, A., *Coco Chanel* (Holmes & Meier, 1992)

Mears, P., 'The Arc of Modernity I: Women's Couture in the 1930s', in Mears and Boyer (eds), *Elegance in the Age of Crisis: Fashions of the 1930s* (Yale University Press, 2014)

Mears, P., 'The Arc of Modernity II: London, New York, Hollywood, Shanghai', in Mears and Boyer (eds), *Elegance in the Age of Crisis: Fashions of the 1930s* (Yale University Press, 2014)

Mears, P., Boyer, G.B., *Elegance in the Age of Crisis: Fashions of the 1930s* (Yale University Press, 2014)

Merceron, D., *Lanvin* (Rizzoli International, 2007)

Muller, F., *Art and Fashion* (Thames & Hudson, 2000)

Phipps, C., Reed, C., *Making Vintage Wedding Dresses: Inspiring Timeless Style* (Crowood, 2017)

Steele, V., *Paris Fashion: A Cultural History* (Berg, 1988)

Wilson, E., *Adorned in Dreams: Fashion and Modernity* (Virago, 1987)

Index